P9-EKS-610

BEING IN LOVE

More OSHO Books

Insights for a New Way of Living Series

Awareness
Compassion
Courage
Creativity
Freedom
Intelligence
Intimacy
Intuition
Joy
Maturity

Other Books

Emotional Wellness
The Book of Understanding
Autobiography of a Spiritually Incorrect Mystic
The Book of Secrets
Pharmacy for the Soul
Love, Freedom, Aloneness
Meditation: The First and Last Freedom
Sex Matters
Your Answers Questioned
Osho Transformation Tarot
Osho Zen Tarot
Tao: The Pathless Path
Zen: The Path of Paradox
Yoga: The Science of the Soul
Tarot in the Spirit of Zen
Meditation for Busy People
Body Mind Balancing
The ABC of Enlightenment

Audio

Book of Secrets: Keys to Love and Meditation
Ah, This! The Heart Sutra
Osho Meditations on Buddhism
Osho Meditations on Tantra
Osho Meditations on Tao
Osho Meditations on Yoga
Osho Meditations on Zen

How to love
with awareness and
relate without fear

BEING IN LOVE

Harmony Books
New York

Published in the United States by Harmony Books, an imprint of the Crown Publishing Group, a division of Random House, Inc., New York.
www.crownpublishing.com

Harmony Books is a registered trademark and the Harmony Books colophon is a trademark of Random House, Inc.

OSHO is a registered trademark of Osho International Foundation, used with permission/license.

The material in this book is selected from various discourses by Osho given to a live audience. All of the Osho discourses have been published in full as books and are also available as original audio recordings. Audio recordings and the complete text archive can be found via the online OSHO Library at www.osho.com.

Library of Congress Cataloging-in-Publication Data
Osho, 1931–1990.
Being in love : how to love with awareness and relate without fear / Osho.—1st ed.
p. cm.
1. Love—Religious aspects. I. Title.
BP605.R34B445 2008
299'.93—dc22 2007036736

ISBN 978-0-307-33790-0

Printed in the United States of America

Designed by Barbara Sturman

10 9

CONTENTS

BEING IN LOVE

INTRODUCTION: WHAT IS LOVE?

It is unfortunate that we have to ask this question. In the natural course of things everybody would know what love is. But in fact nobody knows, or only very rarely does somebody know, what love is. Love has become one of the rarest experiences. Yes, it is talked about. Films and stories are written about it, songs are composed about it, on the television shows you will see it, on the radio, in magazines—a great industry exists to supply you with ideas of what love is. Many people are involved in the industry of helping people understand what love is. But still love remains an unknown phenomenon. And it should be one of the most known.

It is almost like somebody asking, "What is food?" Would you not be surprised if somebody came and asked you that question? Only if somebody has been starved from the very beginning and has never tasted food would the question be relevant. It is the same with the question "What is love?"

Love is the food of the soul, but you have been starved. Your soul has not received love at all, so you don't know the taste. So the question is relevant, but it is unfortunate. The body has received food so the body continues; but the soul has not received food so the soul is dead, or is not born yet, or is always on its deathbed.

When we are born we are born fully equipped with the capacity to love and to be loved. Each child is born full of love and knows perfectly what it is. There is no need to tell a child what love is. But the problem arises because the mother and the father don't know what love is. No child receives the parents that he deserves—no child ever receives the parents that he deserves; those parents simply don't exist on the earth. And by the time this child becomes a parent, he too will have lost the capacity to love.

I have heard about a small valley where children were born

and within three months they all became blind. It was a small, primitive society, and a fly existed there which caused an infection and blindness in the eyes, so the whole community had gone blind. Every child was born with eyes that functioned perfectly well, but within three months at the most they had gone blind because of these flies. Now, somewhere later in life those children must have asked, "What are eyes? What do you mean when you use the word 'eye'? What is vision? What is seeing? What do you mean?" And the question would have been relevant. Those children had been born with sight, but they had lost it somewhere on the way of their growth.

That's what has happened to love. Every child is born with as much love as one can contain, with more love than one can contain, with overflowing love. A child is born as love; a child is made of the stuff called love. But the parents cannot give love. They have their own hangovers—their parents never loved them. The parents can only pretend. They can talk about love. They can say, "We love you very much," but what they actually do is unloving. The way they behave, the way they treat the child is insulting; there is no respect. No parent respects the child. Who ever thinks of respecting a child? A child is not thought to be a person at all. A child is thought of as a problem. If he keeps quiet, he is good; if he does not scream or cause any mischief, good; if he simply keeps out of the parents' way, perfectly good. That's what a child should be. But there is no respect and there is no love.

The parents have not known what love is. The wife has not loved the husband, the husband has not loved the wife. Love does not exist between them—instead there is domination, possessiveness, jealousy, and all kinds of poisons that destroy love. Just as a certain poison can destroy your vision, so the poison of possessiveness and jealousy destroys love.

Love is a fragile flower. It has to be protected, it has to be strengthened, it has to be watered; only then does it become strong. And the child's love is very fragile—naturally, because the child is fragile, his body is fragile. Do you think a child left on his own will be able to survive? Just think how helpless the human child is—if a child is left on his own, it is next to impossible that he will survive. He will die, and that is what is happening to love. Love is left alone, untended.

The parents can't love, they don't know what love is, they have never flowed in love. Just think of your own parents—and remember, I am not saying that they are responsible. They are victims just as you are victims; their own parents were the same. And so on . . . you can go back to Adam and Eve and God the father! It seems that even God the father was not very respectful to Adam and Eve. That's why from the very beginning he started commanding them, "Do this" and "Don't do that." He started doing the same rubbish that all parents do. "Don't eat the fruit of this tree." And when Adam had eaten the fruit, the father God was so angry in reaction that he threw Adam and Eve out of heaven.

That expulsion is always there, and each parent threatens to expel the child, to throw him out. "If you don't listen, if you don't behave, you will be thrown out." Naturally the child is afraid. Thrown out? Into the wilderness of this life? He starts compromising. The child by and by becomes twisted, and he starts manipulating. He does not want to smile, but if the mother is nearby and he wants milk, he smiles. Now this is politics—the beginning, the ABC of politics.

Deep down the child starts hating the parents because he is not respected; deep down he starts feeling frustrated because he is not loved as he is. He is expected to do certain things, and only then will he be loved. Love has conditions; he is not worthy as he is. First he has to become worthy, only then will the parents' love be given. So to become "worthy" the child starts becoming false; he loses any sense of his own intrinsic value. His respect for himself is lost, and by and by he starts feeling that he is guilty.

Many times the idea comes to the mind of a child, "Are these my real parents? Is it possible they have adopted me? Maybe they are deceiving me, because there seems to be no love." A thousand and one times he sees the anger in their eyes, the ugly anger on the faces of his parents, and for such small things that he cannot understand the proportion of anger caused by these small things. Just for very small things he sees the parents' rage—he cannot believe it, it is so unjust and unfair! But he has to surrender, he has to bow down, he has to accept it as a necessity. By and by, his capacity for love is killed.

Love grows only in love. Love needs a milieu of love—that is the most fundamental thing to be remembered. Only in a milieu of love does love grow; it needs the same kind of pulsation around. If the mother is loving, if the father is loving—not only to the child, if they are loving to each other too, if the home has an atmosphere where love flows—the child will start functioning as a love-being, and he will never ask the question, "What is love?" He will know it from the very beginning, it will become his foundation.

But that doesn't happen. It is unfortunate, but it has not happened up to now. And children learn the ways of their parents—their nagging, their conflict. Just go on watching yourself. If you are a woman, watch—you may be repeating, almost identically, the ways your mother used to behave. Watch yourself when you are with your boyfriend or your husband: What are you doing? Are you not repeating a pattern? If you are a man, watch: What are you doing? Are you not behaving just like your father? Are you not doing the same nonsense that he used to do? Once upon a time you were surprised—"How can my father do this?"—and now you are doing the same. People go on repeating; people are imitators. The human being is a monkey. You are repeating your father or your mother, and that has to be dropped. Only then will you know what love is, otherwise you will remain corrupted.

I cannot define what love is because there is no definition of love. It is one of those indefinables like birth, like death, like God, like meditation. It is one of those indefinables—I cannot define it. I cannot say that "this is love," I cannot show it to you. It is not a visible phenomenon. It cannot be dissected, cannot be analyzed; it can only be experienced, and only through experience do you know what it is. But I can show you the way to experience it.

The first step is, get rid of your parents. And by that I don't mean any disrespect toward your parents, no. I will be the last person to say that. And I don't mean you should get rid of your physical parents, I mean you have to get rid of your parental voices inside, your program inside, your tapes inside. Efface them . . . and you will be simply surprised that if you get rid of your parents from your inner being, you become free. For the first time you will be able to feel compassion for your parents, otherwise not; you will remain resentful.

Every person feels resentful toward his or her parents. How can you not be resentful when they have done so much harm to you? And they have not harmed you knowingly—they wished all good for you, they wanted to do everything for your well-being. But what can they do? Just by wanting something, it doesn't happen. Just by good wishes, nothing happens. They were well-wishers, that is true; there is no doubt about it; every parent wants the child to have all the joys of life. But what can they do? They have not known any joy themselves. They are robots, and knowingly, or unknowingly, deliberately or unintentionally, they will create an atmosphere in which their children will sooner or later be turned into robots.

If you want to become a human being and not a machine, get rid of your parents. And you will have to be watchful. It is hard work, arduous work; you cannot do it instantly. You will have to be very careful in your behavior. Watch and see when your mother is there, functioning through you—stop that, move away from it. Do something absolutely new that your mother could not even have imagined. For example, your boyfriend is looking at some other woman with great appreciation in his eyes. Now, watch what you are doing. Are you doing the same as your mother would have done when your father looked at another woman appreciatively? If you do that, you will never know what love is, you will simply be repeating a story. It will be the same act being played by different actors, that's all; the same rotten act being repeated again and again and again. Don't be an imitator, get out of it. Do something new. Do something that your mother could not have conceived of. Do something new that your father could not have conceived of. This newness has to be brought to your being, then your love will start flowing.

So the first essential is getting rid of your parents.

The second essential is this: People think that they can love only when they find a worthy partner—nonsense! You will never find one. People think they will love only when they find a perfect man or a perfect woman. Nonsense! You will never find them, because perfect women and perfect men don't exist. And if they exist, they won't bother about your love. They will not be interested.

I have heard about a man who remained a bachelor his whole life because he was in search of a perfect woman. When he was seventy, somebody asked, "You have been traveling and traveling—from New York to Kathmandu, from Kathmandu to Rome, from Rome to London you have been searching. Could you not find a perfect woman? Not even one?"

The old man became very sad. He said, "Yes, once I did. One day, long ago, I came across a perfect woman."

The inquirer said, "Then what happened? Why didn't you get married?"

Sadly, the old man said, "What to do? She was looking for a perfect man."

And remember, when two beings are perfect, their love need is not the same as your love need. It has a totally different quality.

You don't understand even the love that is possible for you, so you will not be able to understand the love that happens to a Buddha, or the love that is flowing from a Lao Tzu toward you—you will not be able to understand it.

First you have to understand the love that is a natural phenomenon. Even that has not happened. First you have to understand the natural, and then the transcendental. So the second thing to remember is, never be in search of a perfect man or a perfect woman. That idea too has been put into your mind—that unless you find a perfect man or a perfect woman you will not be happy. So you go on looking for the perfect, and you don't find it, so you are unhappy.

To flow and grow in love needs no perfection. Love has nothing to do with the other. A loving person simply loves, just as an alive person breathes and drinks and eats and sleeps. Exactly like that, a really alive person, a loving person, loves. You don't say, "Unless there is perfect air, unpolluted, I am not going to breathe." You go on breathing even in Los Angeles; you go on breathing in Mumbai. You go on breathing everywhere, even when the air is polluted, poisoned. You go on breathing! You cannot afford not to breathe just because the air is not as it should be. If you are hungry you eat something, whatever it is. In a desert, if you are dying of thirst you will drink anything. You will not insist on having Coca-Cola, anything will do—any drink, just water, even dirty water. People are known to have drunk their own urine. When one is dying of thirst one does not bother with what it is, one will drink anything to quench the thirst. People have killed their camels in the desert to drink water—because camels store water inside them. Now this is dangerous, because now the person will have to walk for miles. But they are so thirsty that first things come first—first the water; otherwise they will die. Without water, even if the camel is still there, what are they going to do? The camel will have to take a corpse to the next town, because without water they will die.

An alive and loving person simply loves. Love is a natural function.

So the second thing to remember is, don't ask for perfection; otherwise you will not find any love flowing in you. On the contrary, you will become *un*loving. People who demand perfection are very unloving people, neurotic. Even if they can find a lover they demand perfection, and the love is destroyed because of that demand.

Once a man loves a woman or a woman loves a man, demands immediately enter. The woman starts demanding that the man should be perfect, just because he loves her. As if he has committed a sin! Now he has to be perfect, now he has to drop all his limitations—suddenly, just because of this woman? Now he cannot be human? Either he has to become superhuman or he has to become phony, false, a cheat.

Naturally, to become superhuman is very difficult, so people become cheats. They start pretending and acting and playing games. In the name of love people are just playing games. So the second thing to remember is never to demand perfection. You have no right to demand anything from anybody. If somebody loves you, be thankful, but don't demand anything—because the other has no obligation to love you. If somebody loves, it is a miracle. Be thrilled by the miracle.

But people are not thrilled. For small things they will destroy all possibilities of love. They are not interested much in love and the joy of it. They are more interested in other ego trips.

Be concerned with your joy. Be utterly concerned with your joy, be *only* concerned with your joy. Everything else is non-essential. Love—as a natural function, just as you breathe. And when you love a person, don't start demanding; otherwise from the very beginning you are closing the doors. Don't expect anything. If something comes your way, feel grateful. If nothing comes, there is no need for it to come, there is no necessity for it to come. You cannot expect it.

But watch people, see how they take each other for granted. If your wife prepares food for you, you never thank her. I'm not saying that you have to verbalize your thanks, but it should be in your eyes. But you don't bother, you take it for granted—that is her work. Who told you that?

If your husband goes and earns money, you never thank him. You don't feel any gratitude. "That's what a man should do." That's your mind. How can love grow? Love needs a climate of love, love needs a climate of gratitude, thankfulness. Love needs a non-demanding atmosphere, non-expecting atmosphere. This is the second thing to remember.

And the third thing is: Rather than thinking how to get love, start giving. If you give, you get. There is no other way. People are more interested in how to grab and get. Everybody is interested in getting and nobody seems to enjoy giving. People give very reluctantly—if ever they give, they give only to get, and they are almost businesslike. It is a bargain. They always go on watching to make sure they get more than they give—then it is a good bargain, good business. And the other is doing the same.

Love is not a business, so stop being businesslike. Otherwise you will miss your life and love and all that is beautiful in it—because all that is beautiful is not at all businesslike. Business is the ugliest thing in the world—a necessary evil, but existence knows nothing of business. Trees bloom, it is not a business; the stars shine, it is not a business and you don't have to pay for it and nobody demands anything from you. A bird comes and sits at your door and sings a song, and the bird will not ask you for a certificate or some sign of appreciation. He has sung the song and then happily he flies away, leaving no traces behind.

That's how love grows. Give, and don't wait to see how much you can grab. Yes, it comes, it comes a thousandfold, but it comes naturally. It comes on its own, there is no need to demand it. When you demand, it never comes. When you demand, you have killed it. So give. Start giving.

In the beginning it will be hard, because your whole life you have been trained not to give but to get. In the beginning you will have to fight with your own armor. Your musculature has become hard, your heart has become frozen, you have become cold. In the beginning it will be difficult, but each step will lead to a further step, and by and by the river starts flowing.

First get rid of your parents. In getting rid of your parents you get rid of society, in getting rid of your parents you get rid of civilization, education, everything—because your parents represent all that. You become an individual. For the first time you are no longer part of the mass, you have an authentic individuality. You are on your own. This is what growth is. This is what a grown-up person should be.

A grown-up person is one who needs no parents. A grown-up person is one who needs nobody to cling to or lean upon. A grown-up person is one who is happy in his aloneness—his aloneness is a song, a celebration. A grown-up person is one who can be with himself happily. His aloneness is not loneliness, his solitariness is solitude, it is meditative.

One day you had to come out of your mother's womb. If you had remained there longer than nine months you would have been dead—not only you, your mother would also have been dead. One day you had to come out of your mother's womb; then one day you had to come out of your family atmosphere, another womb, to go to school. Then one day you had to come out of your school atmosphere, another womb, to go into the larger world. But deep down you are still a child. You are still in the womb! Layers upon layers of womb are there and that womb has to be broken.

This is what in the East we have called the second birth. When you have attained to a second birth, you are completely free of parental impressions. And the beauty is that only such a person feels grateful to the parents. The paradox is that only such a person can forgive his parents. He feels compassion and love for them, he feels tremendously for them because they have also suffered in the same way. He is not angry, no, not at all. He may have tears in his eyes but he is not angry, and he will do everything to help his parents to move toward such a plenitude of aloneness, such a height of aloneness.

Become individuals, that's the first thing. The second thing is, don't expect perfection and don't ask and don't demand. Love ordinary people. Nothing is wrong with ordinary people. Ordinary people are extraordinary! Each human being is so unique; have respect for that uniqueness.

Third, give, and give without any condition—then you will know what love is. I cannot define it. I can show you the path to grow it. I can show you how to put in a rosebush, how to water it, how to give fertilizers to it, how to protect it. Then one day, out of the blue, comes the rose, and your home is full of the fragrance. That's how love happens.

PART I

The Journey from "Me" to "We"

Understanding the Nature and Nurture of Love

Love cannot be learned, it cannot be cultivated. The cultivated love will not be love at all. It will not be a real rose, it will be a plastic flower. When you learn something, it means something comes from the outside; it is not an inner growth. And love has to be your inner growth if it is to be authentic and real.

Love is not a learning but a growth. What is needed on your part is not to learn the ways of love but to unlearn the ways of un-love. The hindrances have to be removed, the obstacles have to be destroyed—then love is your natural, spontaneous being. Once the obstacles are removed, the rocks thrown out of the way, the flow starts. It is already there—hidden behind many rocks, but the spring of love is already there. It is your very being.

BEYOND DEPENDENCY AND DOMINATION

Breaking Out of the Shell of the Ego

I have been always surprised by the number of people who come to me and say they are afraid of love. What is the fear of love? It is because when you really love somebody your ego starts slipping away and melting. You cannot love with the ego; the ego becomes a barrier, and when you want to drop the barrier between yourself and the other, the ego says, "This is going to be a death. Beware!"

The death of the ego is not your death; the death of the ego is really your possibility of life. The ego is just a dead crust around you, it has to be broken and thrown away. It comes into being naturally—just as a traveler collects dust on his clothes, on his body, and he has to take a bath to get rid of the dust. As we move through time, the dust of our experiences, our knowledge, of the life we have lived, of the past, collects. That dust becomes the ego. It accumulates and becomes a crust around you, which has to be broken and thrown away. One has to take a bath every day, in fact every moment, so that this crust never becomes a prison.

It will be helpful to understand where the ego comes from, to understand the roots.

A child is born and is absolutely helpless, particularly the human child. He cannot survive without others' help. Most children of the animals, the trees, the birds, can survive without the parents, can survive without a society, without a family. Even if sometimes help is needed, it is very little—a few days, at the most a few months. But a human child is so helpless that he has to depend on others for years. It is there that the root has to be sought.

Why does helplessness create the human ego? The child is helpless, he depends on others, but the ignorant mind of the child interprets this dependence as if he is the center of the whole world. The child thinks, "Whenever I cry, my mother runs immediately; whenever I am hungry, I just have to give an indication and the breast is given. Whenever I am wet, just a slight cry and somebody comes and changes my clothes." The child lives like an emperor. In fact he is absolutely helpless and dependent, and the mother and father, the family and his caretakers, are all helping him to survive. They are not dependent on the child, the child is dependent on them. But the mind of the child interprets this as if he is the center of the whole world, as if the whole world exists just for him.

And the world of the child is, of course, very small in the beginning. It consists of the mother, the caretaker, the father on the fringe—this is the child's whole world. These people love the child. And the child becomes more and more egoistic. He feels himself to be the very center of all existence, and in that way the ego is created. Through dependence and helplessness, the ego is created.

In fact the child's real situation is just the contrary from what he thinks; there is no real justification to create such an ego. But the child is absolutely ignorant, he is not capable of understanding the complexity of the thing. He cannot know that he is helpless, he thinks he is the dictator! And then for his whole life he will try to remain the dictator. He will become a Napoleon, an Alexander, an Adolf Hitler—your presidents, prime ministers, dictators, are all childish. They are trying to achieve the same thing they experienced as children; they want to be the center of the whole existence. With them the world should live and die; the whole world is their periphery and they are the center of it; the very meaning of life is hidden in them.

The child, of course, naturally finds this interpretation correct, because when the mother looks at him, in the eyes of the mother he sees that he is the significance of her life. When the father comes home, the child feels that he is the very meaning of the father's life. This lasts for three or four years—and the years at the beginning of life are the most important; never again will there be a time in a person's life with the same potential.

Psychologists say that after the first four years the child is almost complete. The whole pattern is fixed; throughout the rest of life you will repeat the same pattern in different situations. And by the seventh year the child has all his attitudes confirmed, his ego is settled. Now he moves out into the world—and then everywhere he encounters problems, millions of problems! Once you are out of the circle of the family, problems will arise—because nobody else bothers about you in the same way your mother bothered about you; nobody is as concerned about you as your father was. Instead, everywhere you find indifference, and the ego is hurt.

But now the pattern is set. Whether it hurts or not, the child cannot change the pattern—it has become the very blueprint of his being. He will play with other children and try to dominate them. He will go to school and try to dominate, to come first in his class, to become the most important student. He might believe he is superior but he finds that all the other children believe the same way. There is conflict, there are egos, there is fighting, struggle.

Then this becomes the whole story of life: there are millions of egos around you, just like yours, and everybody is trying to control, maneuver, dominate—through wealth, power, politics, knowledge, strength, lies, pretensions, hypocrisies. Even in religion and morality, everybody is trying to dominate, to show the rest of the world that "I am the center of the world."

This is the root of all problems between people. Because of this concept, you are always in conflict and struggle with somebody or other. Not that others are enemies to you—everybody else is just like you, in the same boat. The situation is the same for everybody else; they have been brought up in the same way.

There exists a certain school of psychoanalysts in the West who have proposed that unless children are brought up without their fathers and mothers, the world will never be at peace. I don't support them, because then children will never be brought up in any way! Those psychologists have something of truth in their proposal, but it is a very dangerous idea. Because if children are brought up in nurseries without fathers and mothers, without any love, with total indifference, they may not have the problems of the ego but they will have other, even more damaging and dangerous problems.

If a child is brought up in total indifference he will have no center. He will be a hotchpotch, clumsy, not knowing who he is. He will not have any identity. Afraid, scared, he will not be able to take even a single step without fear, because nobody has loved him. Of course, the ego will not be there, but without it he will have no center. He will not become a buddha; he will be just dull and crippled, always feeling afraid.

Love is needed to make you feel fearless, to make you feel that you are accepted, that you are not useless, that you cannot be discarded in the junkyard. If children are brought up in a situation where love is lacking, they will not have egos, that's true. Their life will not have so much struggle and fight. But they will not be able to stand up for themselves at all. They will be always in flight, escaping from everybody, hiding in caves in their own being. They will not be buddhas, they will not be radiant with vitality, they will not be centered, at ease, at home. They will simply be eccentric, off-center. That will not be a good situation either.

So I don't support these psychologists. Their approach would create robots, not human beings—and robots of course have no problems. Or, they may create human beings who are more like animals. There will be less anxiety, less ulcers, less cancer, but that is not worth achieving when it means that you cannot grow to a higher peak of consciousness. Instead you would be falling downward; it will be a regression. Of course, if you become an animal there will be less anguish, because there will be less consciousness. And if you become a stone, a rock, there will be no anxiety at all because there is nobody inside to feel anxious, to feel anguish. But this is not worth achieving. One has to be like a god, not like a rock. And by that I mean it to have absolute consciousness and still have no worries, no anxieties, no problems; to enjoy life like the birds, to celebrate life like birds, to sing like birds—not through regression but by growing to the optimum of consciousness.

The child gathers ego—it is natural, nothing can be done about it. One has to accept it. But later on, there is no need to keep carrying it. That ego is needed in the beginning for the child to feel that he is accepted, loved, welcomed—that he is an invited guest, not an accident. The father, the mother, the family, and the warmth around the child help him to grow strong, rooted, grounded. It is needed, the ego gives him protection—it is good, it is just like the shell of a seed. But the shell should not become the ultimate thing, otherwise the seed will die. The protection can go on too long, then it becomes a prison. The protection must remain a protection while it is needed, and when the moment comes for the hard shell of the seed to die into the earth, it should die naturally so that the seed can sprout and life can be born.

The ego is just a protective shell—the child needs it because he is helpless. The child needs it because he is weak; the child needs it because he is vulnerable and there are millions of forces all around. He needs protection, a home, a base. The whole world may be indifferent but he can always look toward home, and from there he can gather significance.

But, with significance comes the ego. The child becomes egoistic, and with this ego arise all the problems you face. This ego will not allow you to fall in love. This ego would like everybody to surrender to you; it will not allow you to surrender to anybody—and love happens only when *you* surrender. When you force somebody else to surrender it is hateful, destructive. It is not love. And if there is no love, your life will be without warmth, without any poetry in it. It may be prose, mathematical, logical, rational. But how can one live without poetry?

Prose is okay, rationality is okay, it is utilitarian, needed—but living just through reason and logic can never be a celebration, can never be festive. And when life is not festive, it is boring. Poetry is needed—but for poetry you need surrender. You need to throw off this ego. If you can do it, if you can put it aside even for a few moments, your life will have glimpses of the beautiful, of the divine.

Without poetry you cannot really live, you can only exist. Love is poetry. And if love is not possible, how can you be prayerful, meditative, aware? It becomes almost impossible. And without a meditative awareness, you will remain just a body; you will never become aware of the innermost soul. Only in prayerfulness, in a deep meditation and silence do you reach the peaks. That prayerful silence, that meditative awareness is the highest peak of experience—but love opens the door.

Carl Gustav Jung, after a lifetime of studying thousands of people—thousands of cases of people who were ill, psychologically crippled, psychologically confused—said that he had never come across a psychologically ill person whose real problem after the fortieth year is not spiritual. There is a rhythm in life, and in your forties a new dimension arises, the spiritual dimension. If you cannot tackle it rightly, if you don't know what to do, you will become ill, you will become restless. The whole of human growth is a continuity. If you miss one step, it becomes discontinuous. The child gathers ego—and if he never learns to put the ego aside he cannot love, cannot be at ease with anybody. The ego will be constantly in fight. You may be sitting silently, but the ego is constantly fighting, just looking out for ways to dominate, to be dictatorial, to become the ruler of the world.

This creates problems everywhere. In friendship, sex, love, in the society—everywhere you are in conflict. There is even conflict with the parents who have given this ego to you. It is rare that a son forgives his father, rare that a woman forgives her mother. It happens very rarely.

George Gurdjieff had a sentence on the wall of the room where he used to meet with people. The sentence was this: "If you are not yet at ease with your father and mother, then go away. I cannot help you." Why? Because the problem has arisen there and it has to be solved there. That's why all the old traditions say love your parents, respect your parents as deeply as possible—because the ego arises there, that is the soil. Solve it there, otherwise it will haunt you everywhere.

Psychoanalysts have also come to the conclusion that all they do is bring you back to the problems that existed between you and your parents and try to solve them somehow. If you can solve your conflict with your parents, many other conflicts will simply disappear because they are based on the same fundamental conflict.

For example, a man who is not at ease with his father cannot be at ease with the boss in the office—never, because the boss is a father figure. That small conflict with your parents continues to be reflected in all your relationships. If you are not at ease with your mother, you cannot be at ease with your wife because she will be the representative woman; you cannot be at ease with women as such, because your mother is the first woman, she is the first model of a woman. Wherever a woman is, your mother is, and a subtle relationship continues.

Ego is born in the relationship with the father and mother, and it has to be tackled there. Otherwise you will go on cutting branches and leaves of the tree, and the root remains untouched. If you have settled with your father and mother, you have become mature. Now there is no ego. Now you understand that you were helpless, now you understand that you depended on others, that you were not the center of the world. In fact, you were completely dependent; you could not have survived otherwise. Understanding this, the ego by and by fades and, once you are not in conflict with life, you become loose and natural, you relax. Then you float. Then the world is not filled with enemies, it is a family, an organic unity. The world is not against you, you can float with it. Finding that the ego is nonsense, finding that the ego has no grounds to exist, finding that the ego is just a childish dream, misconceived in ignorance, one simply becomes egoless.

There are people who come to me and they ask, "How to fall in love? Is there a way?" How to fall in love? They ask for a way, a method, a certain technique.

They don't understand what they are asking. Falling in love

means that now there is no way, no technique, no method. That's why it is called "falling in"—you are no longer the controller, you simply fall in. That's why people who are very head-oriented will say love is blind. Love is the only eye, the only vision—but they will say love is blind, and if you are in love they will think you have gone mad. It looks mad to the head-oriented person, because the mind is a great manipulator. Any situation in which control is lost looks dangerous to the mind.

But there is a world of the human heart, there is a world of the human being and consciousness where no technique is possible. All technologies are possible with matter; with consciousness no technologies are possible and in fact, no control is possible. The very effort to control or to make a thing happen is egoistic.

THE NATURAL STAGES OF LIFE AND LOVING

People have asked me, what is the right way to provide a loving atmosphere that can help a child grow without interfering in his natural potentiality.

Every way to help a child is wrong. The very idea of helping is not right. The child needs your love, not your help. The child needs nourishment, support, but not your help. The natural potential of the child is unknown, so there is no way to help him rightly to attain his natural potential. You cannot help when the goal is unknown; all that you can do is not interfere. And in fact, in the name of "help" everybody is interfering with everybody else; and because the name is beautiful, nobody objects. Of course the child is so small, so dependent on you, he cannot object.

All the people around are just like you: they have also been helped by their parents, the way you have been helped. Neither they have attained their natural potential, nor have you. The whole world is missing out in spite of all the help from parents, from the family, from relatives, from the neighbors, teachers, priests. In fact everybody is so burdened with help that under its weight, what to say of attaining natural potential, one cannot even attain unnatural potential! One cannot move; the weight on everybody's shoulders is Himalayan.

All the people around you have been helped, greatly helped to be what they are. You have been helped; now you want to help the children, too? All that you can do is to be loving, nourishing. Be warm, be accepting. The child brings an unknown potential, and there is no way to figure out what he is going to be. So there is no possibility to suggest, "In this way you should help the child." Each child is unique, so there cannot be a general discipline for every child.

The right way is not to help the child at all. If you have real courage then please don't help the child. Love him, nourish him. Let him do what he wants to do. Let him go where he wants to go. Your mind will be tempted again and again to interfere, and with good excuses. The mind is very clever in rationalizing: "If you don't interfere there may be danger; the child may fall into the well if you don't stop him." But I say to you, it is better to let him fall into the well than to help him and destroy him.

It is a very rare possibility that the child falls into the well—and then too, it does not mean death; he can be taken out. And if you are really so concerned, the well can be covered; but don't help the child, and don't interfere. The well can be fenced, but don't interfere with the child. Your real concern should be to remove all dangers but don't interfere with the child; let him go on his way.

You will have to understand some significant growth patterns. Life has seven-year cycles, it moves in seven-year cycles just as the earth makes one rotation on its axis in twenty-four hours. Now nobody knows why not twenty-five, why not twenty-three. There is no way to answer it; it is simply a fact. So don't ask me why life moves in seven-year cycles. I don't know. This much I know, that it moves in seven-year cycles, and if you understand those cycles you will understand a great deal about human growth.

The first seven years are the most important because the foundation of life is being laid. That's why all the religions are very much concerned about grabbing children as quickly as possible. Those first seven years are the years when you are conditioned, stuffed with all kinds of ideas which will go on haunting you your whole life, which will go on distracting you from your potentiality, which will corrupt you, which will never allow you to see clearly. They will always come like clouds before your eyes and they will make everything confused.

Things are clear, very clear—existence is absolutely clear—but your eyes have gathered layers upon layers of dust. And all that dust has been arranged in the first seven years of your life when you were so innocent, so trusting, that whatsoever was told to you, you accepted as truth. And whatever has gone into your foundation, later on it will be very difficult for you to uncover: it has become almost part of your blood, bones, your very marrow. You will ask a thousand other questions but you will never ask about the basic foundations of your belief.

The first expression of love toward the child is to leave his first seven years absolutely innocent, unconditioned, to leave him for seven years completely wild, a pagan. He should not be converted to Hinduism, to Mohammedanism, to Christianity. Anybody who is trying to convert a child to some religion is not compassionate, he is cruel: he is contaminating the very soul of a new, fresh arrival. Before the child has even asked questions he has been answered with ready-made philosophies, dogmas, ideologies. This is a very strange situation. The child has not asked about God, and you go on teaching him about God. Why so much impatience? Wait!

If the child someday shows interest in God and starts asking, then try to tell him not only your idea of God—because nobody has any monopoly. Put before him all the ideas of God that have been presented to different people by different ages, by different religions, cultures, civilizations. Put before him all the ideas about God, and tell him, "You can choose among these, whichever appeals to you. Or you can invent your own, if nothing suits you. If everything seems to be flawed, and you think you can come up with a better idea, then invent your own. Or if you find that there is no way to invent an idea without loopholes, then drop the whole thing; there is no need."

A person can live without God; there is no intrinsic necessity. Millions of people have lived without God, so God is nothing that is inevitably needed by anybody. You can tell the child, "Yes, I have my idea; and that too is in the combination of all sorts of ideas in this collection. You can choose that, but I am not saying that my idea is the right idea. It appeals to me; it may not appeal to you."

There is no inner necessity that the son should agree with the father, the daughter should agree with the mother. In fact it seems far better that children should *not* agree with the parents. That's how evolution happens. If every child agrees with the father then there will be no evolution, because each new father will agree with his own father, and everybody will be where God left Adam and Eve—naked, outside the gate of the Garden of Eden. Everybody will be stuck there.

Because sons and daughters have disagreed with their fathers and mothers, with their whole tradition, human beings have evolved. This whole evolution is a tremendous disagreement with the past. And the more intelligent you are, the more you are going to disagree. But parents appreciate the child who agrees and they condemn the child who disagrees.

Up to seven years, if a child can be left innocent, uncorrupted by the ideas of others, then to distract him from his potential growth becomes impossible. The child's first seven years are the most vulnerable. And they are in the hands of parents, teachers, priests. How to save children from parents, priests, teachers is a question of such enormous importance that it seems almost impossible to find out how to do it. It is not a question of helping the child. It is a question of protecting the child. If you have a child, protect the child from yourself. Protect the child from others who can influence him: at least up to the age of seven years, protect him. The child is just like a small plant, weak, soft; just a strong wind can destroy it, any animal can eat it up. You can put a protective fencing around it but that is not imprisoning, you are simply protecting. When the plant is bigger, the fencing will be removed.

Protect the child from every kind of influence so that he can remain himself and it is only a question of seven years, because then the first cycle will be complete. By seven years he will be well grounded, centered, strong enough. You don't know how strong a seven-year-old child can be because you have not seen uncorrupted children; you have seen only corrupted children. They carry the fears, the cowardliness of their fathers, their mothers, their families. They are not their own selves.

If a child remains uncorrupted for seven years you will be amazed when you meet such a child. He will be as sharp as a sword. His eyes will be clear, his insight will be clear. And you will see a tremendous strength in him which you cannot find even in a seventy-year-old adult, because the foundations are shaky in that adult.

With a weak foundation, as the building goes on becoming higher and higher, the foundation becomes more and more shaky. So you will see that the older a person becomes, the more afraid. When you are young you may be an atheist; when you become old you start believing in God. Why is that? When you were below thirty you were a hippie. You had the courage to go against the society, to behave in your own way: to have long hair, to have a beard, to roam around the world and take all kinds of risks. But by the time you are forty, all that has disappeared. You will be in some office in a suit, clean shaven, well groomed. Nobody will even be able to recognize that you are an exhippie.

Where have all the hippies disappeared to? First you see them with a great force, then they become just like spent cartridges, impotent, defeated, depressed, trying to make something out of life, feeling that all those years of hippiedom were a waste. Others have gone far ahead: somebody has become the president, somebody has become the governor, and people start thinking, "We were stupid; we were just playing the guitar and the whole world passed us by." They repent. It is really difficult to find an old hippie.

So if you are a parent you will need this much courage not to interfere. Open doors to unknown directions to the child so he can explore. He does not know what he has in him, nobody knows. He has to grope in the dark. Don't make him afraid of darkness, don't make him afraid of failure, don't make him afraid of the unknown. Give him support. When he is going on an unknown journey, send him with all your support, with all your love, with all your blessings. Don't let him be affected by your fears. You may have fears, but keep them to yourself. Don't unload those fears on the child because that will be interfering.

After seven years, the next cycle of seven years, from seven to fourteen, is a new addition to life. The child begins to experience the first stirring of sexual energies. But this is only a kind of rehearsal.

To be a parent is a difficult job, so unless you are ready to take that difficult job, don't become a parent. People simply go on becoming fathers and mothers not knowing what they are doing. You are bringing a new life into existence; all the care in the world will be needed.

Now when the child starts playing out his sexual rehearsals, that is the time when parents interfere the most, because they have been interfered with. All that they know is what has been done to them, so they simply go on doing that to their children. Societies don't allow sexual rehearsal, or at least have not allowed it up to now, and that too only in very advanced countries. Now boys and girls are at least educated in the same schools. But in a country like India, even today in most places coeducation starts only at the university level. The seven-year-old boy and the seven-year-old girl cannot be in the same boarding school. And this is the time for them—without any risk, without the girl getting pregnant, without any problems arising for their families—this is the time when they should be allowed all playfulness. Yes, it will have a sexual color to it, but it is rehearsal; it is not the real drama. And if you don't allow them even the rehearsal and then suddenly one day the curtain opens, and the real drama starts! The actors don't know what is going on; not even a prompter is there to tell them what to do. You have messed up their lives completely.

Those seven years in the second cycle in life are significant as a time for rehearsal. Children will meet, mix, play, become acquainted. And that will help humanity to drop almost 90 percent of its perversions. If children from seven to fourteen are allowed to be together, to swim together, to be naked before each other, 90 percent of perversions and 90 percent of pornography will simply disappear. Who will bother about it? When a boy has known so many girls naked, what interest can a magazine like *Playboy* have for him? When a girl has seen so many boys naked, I don't see that there is any possibility of curiosity about the other; it will simply disappear. They will grow together naturally, not as two different species of animals.

Right now that's how they grow, as if they are two different species of animals. They don't belong to one humankind; they are kept separate. A thousand and one barriers are created between them so they cannot have any rehearsal for their sexual life which is going to come. Because this rehearsal is missing, that's why in people's actual sex life foreplay is missing. And foreplay is so important—far more important than actual sexual contact, because actual sexual contact lasts only for a few moments. It is not nourishment, it simply leaves you in a limbo. You were hoping for so much, and nothing comes out of it.

In Hindi we have a proverb: *Kheela pahad nikli chuhia.* "You dug out the whole mountain and you found one rat." After all the effort—going to the movies and going to the disco, going to the restaurant and talking all kinds on nonsense which neither you nor the other wants to do, but both are talking—digging the mountain, and in the end, just a rat! Nothing is so frustrating as sex.

Just the other day somebody brought me an advertisement for a new car, and in the advertisement they had a beautiful sentence that I liked. The sentence was: "It is better than sex." I don't care about the car, but the advertisement was beautiful! Certainly if you look around you, you will find a thousand and one things better than sex. Sex is just a rat, and that after so much huffing and puffing, so much perspiration, in the end both feel cheated. The reason is that you don't know the art of sex; you know only the middle point. It is as if you see a film just in the middle for a few seconds. Naturally you can't make any sense of it; the beginning is missing and the end is missing. Perhaps you simply saw an interval where there was nothing going on.

The man feels ashamed after sex; he turns over and goes to

sleep. He simply cannot face the woman. He feels ashamed, that's why he turns to his side and goes to sleep. The woman weeps and cries because this was not what she was hoping for. This is all? Then what is this whole drama all about? But the reason is because the rehearsal part of your life has been canceled by your society. You don't know what foreplay is.

Foreplay is really the most satisfying part in sex. Foreplay is more loving. Sex is simply a biological climax, but the climax of what? You have missed everything that could have made it a climax. Do you think you suddenly reach the climax, missing all the rungs of the ladder? You have to move up the ladder, rung by rung, only then can you reach the climax. Everybody heads straight for the climax.

But most people's sexual life is nothing but a kind of relief. Yes, for a moment you feel relieved of a burden, just like a good sneeze. How good it feels afterwards! But for how long? How long can you feel good after a sneeze? How many seconds, how many minutes can you brag that "I had such a sneeze, it was great." As the sneeze is gone, with it goes all the joy, too. It was simply something bothering you. You are finished with that botheration, now there is a little relaxation. That's the sexual life of most of the people in the world. Some energy was bothering you, was making you heavy; it was turning into a headache. Sex gives you relief.

But the way children are brought up is almost butchering their whole life. Those seven years of sexual rehearsal are absolutely essential. Girls and boys should be together in schools, in hostels, in swimming pools and beds. They should rehearse for the life that is going to come; they have to get ready for it. And there is no danger, there is no problem if a child is given total freedom to explore his growing sexual energy and is not condemned, repressed. But that is what is being done. It is a very strange world in which you are living. You are born of sex, you will live for sex, your children will be born out of sex—and sex is the most condemned thing, the greatest sin. And all your religions go on putting this crap in your mind.

People all around the world are full of everything rotten that you can conceive, for the simple reason that they have not been allowed to grow in the natural way. They have not been allowed to accept themselves. They all have become ghosts. They are not authentically real people, they are only shadows of someone they could have been.

The second cycle of seven years is immensely important because it will prepare you for the coming seven years. If you have done your homework rightly, if you have played with your sexual energy just in the spirit of a sportsman—and during those years, that is the only spirit you will have—you will not become a pervert, and all kinds of strange things will not come to your mind. Instead you will be moving naturally with the other sex, the other sex is moving with you. There will be no hindrance, and you will not be doing anything wrong against anybody. Your conscience will be clear because nobody has put into your head ideas of what is right, what is wrong: you are simply being whatever you are.

Then from fourteen to twenty-one, your sex matures. And this is significant to understand: if the rehearsal has gone well, in the seven years when your sex matures a very strange thing happens that you may not have ever thought about, because you have not been given the chance. I said to you that the second seven-year cycle, from seven to fourteen, gives you a glimpse of foreplay. The third seven-year cycle will give you a glimpse of afterplay. You are still together with girls or boys, but now a new phase starts in your being: you start falling in love.

It is still not a biological interest. You are not interested in producing children, you are not interested in becoming husbands and wives, no. These are the years of romantic play. You are more interested in beauty, in love, in poetry, in sculpture, which are all different phases of romanticism. And unless a person has some romantic quality he will never know what afterplay is. Sex is just in the middle. The longer the foreplay, the better the possibility of reaching the climax; the better the possibility of reaching the climax, the better opening for afterplay. And unless a couple knows afterplay they will never know what sex in its completion is.

Now there are sexologists who are teaching foreplay. A taught foreplay is not the real thing, but they are teaching it; at least they have recognized the fact that without foreplay sex cannot reach the climax. But they are at a loss how to teach afterplay, because when a man has reached the climax he is no longer interested. He is finished, the job is done. For afterplay to happen it needs a romantic mind, a poetic mind, a mind that knows how to be thankful, how to be grateful. The person, the woman or the man who has brought you to such a climax, needs some gratitude: afterplay is your gratitude. And unless there is afterplay it simply means your sex is incomplete; and incomplete sex is the cause of all the troubles that a human being goes through. Sex can become orgasmic only when afterplay and foreplay are completely balanced. Just in their balance the climax turns into orgasm.

And the word "orgasm" has to be understood. It means that your whole being—body, mind, soul, everything—becomes involved, organically involved. Then it becomes a moment of meditation. To me, if your sex does not become finally a moment of meditation, you have not known what sex is. You have only heard about it, you have read about it; and the people who have been writing about it know nothing about it. I have read hundreds of books on sexology by people who are thought to be great experts, and they are "experts," but they know nothing about the innermost shrine where meditation blossoms. Just as children are born from ordinary sex, meditation is born out of extraordinary sex.

Animals can produce children; there is nothing special about it. It is only man who can produce the experience of meditation as the center of his orgasmic feeling. This is possible only if from the ages of fourteen to twenty-one young people are allowed to have romantic freedom.

From twenty-one to twenty-eight is the time when they can settle. They can choose a partner. And they are capable of choosing now; through all the experience of the past two cycles of their growth they can choose the right partner. There is nobody else who can do it for you. It is something that is more like a hunch—not arithmetic, not astrology, not palmistry, not I Ching, nothing else is going to do. It is a hunch. After coming in contact with many, many people, suddenly something clicks that had never clicked with anybody else. And it clicks with so much certainty, and so absolutely, you cannot even doubt it. Even if you try to doubt it, you cannot, the certainty is so tremendous. With this click you settle.

Between twenty-one and twenty-eight—somewhere, if everything goes smoothly in the way I am talking about, without interference from others—then you settle. And the most pleasant period of life comes from twenty-eight to thirty-five—the most joyous, the most peaceful and harmonious, because two persons start melting and merging into each other.

From thirty-five to forty-two, a new step, a new door opens. If up to the age of thirty-five you have felt deep harmony, an orgasmic feeling, and you have discovered meditation through it, then from thirty-five to forty-two you will help each other go more and more into that meditation without sex, because at this point sex starts looking childish, juvenile.

The age of forty-two is the time when a person should be able to know exactly who he is. From forty-two to forty-nine he goes deeper and deeper into meditation, more and more into himself, and helps the partner in the same way. The partners become friends. There is no more "husband" and no more "wife"; that time has passed. It has given its richness to your life; now there is something growing that is even higher than love. That is friendliness, a compassionate relationship to help the other to go deeper into himself or herself, to become more independent, to become more alone, just like two tall trees standing separate but still close to each other, or two pillars in a temple supporting the same roof—standing so close, but also so separate and independent and alone.

From forty-nine to fifty-six this aloneness becomes your focus of being. Everything else in the world loses meaning. The only remaining meaningful thing is this aloneness.

From fifty-six to sixty-three you become absolutely what you are going to become: the potential blossoms, and from sixty-three to seventy you start getting ready to drop the body. Now you know you are not the body, you know you are not the mind either. The body was known as separate from you somewhere around the time when you were thirty-five. That the mind is separate from you was known near the time when you were forty-nine. Now, everything else drops except the witnessing self. Just the pure awareness, the flame of awareness remains with you—and this is the preparation for death.

Seventy is the natural life span for human beings. And if things move in this natural course then one dies with tremendous joy, with great ecstasy, feeling immensely blessed that life has not been meaningless, that at least one has found his home. And because of this richness, this fulfillment, one is capable of blessing the whole of existence. Just to be near such a person at the time of death is a great opportunity. You will feel, as the person leaves the body, as if some invisible flowers are falling upon you. Although you cannot see them, you can feel them. It is sheer joy, so pure that even to have a little taste of it is enough to transform your whole life.

THE CANDLE OF AWARENESS

A questioner has asked, "How to start the journey towards love?" Once you ask the question the journey has already started; you are in the journey. This has to be recognized—unconsciously, you are in the journey: that's why it feels as if you have to start it. Recognize it, become conscious about it, and the very recognition becomes the beginning.

You are always moving, going somewhere—knowingly, unknowingly, willingly, unwillingly, but you are going—some great force is constantly working within you. Existence is evolving, it is constantly creating something within you. So the question is not how to start the journey; the question is how to recognize it. It is there, but your recognition is not there.

For example, trees die, but they don't know that. Birds and animals die, but they don't know. Only human beings know that they have to die, and even that knowledge is very cloudy, not clear. And the same is the case with life—the birds are alive, but they don't know that they are alive. How can you know life if you don't know death? How can you know that you are alive if you don't know that you are going to die? Both recognitions come together. Birds, animals, trees are alive, but they don't recognize that they are alive.

The human being recognizes, a little, that he is going to die, but that recognition remains cloudy, hidden by thick smoke. And the same is true about life: you are alive, but you don't know exactly what being alive means. That too is cloudy, not clear. When I say recognition, I mean becoming alert to what this life energy is, which is already on the way. To become aware of one's own being is the beginning of the journey towards love. To come to a point where you are so absolutely alert that not even a fragment of darkness exists around you is the end of the journey. In fact, the journey never starts and never ends. You will continue even after that, but then the journey will have a totally different meaning, a totally different quality to it: it will be sheer delight. Right now it is sheer misery.

"How to start the journey towards love?" Become more alert about your actions, about your relationships, about your movements. Whatever you do, even an ordinary thing like walking on the street, try to become alert. Try to take your steps with full awareness. Buddha used to say to his disciples: When you take a step with the right foot, remember, now this is the right foot; when you take a step with the left, remember, now this is the left. When you breathe in, remember, "Now I am breathing in." When you breathe out, remember, "Now I am breathing out." Not that you have to verbalize it. Not that you have to say in words "I am breathing in," but just becoming alert that now the breath is going in. I am speaking to you so I have to use words, but when you are becoming alert you need not use words, because words are part of the smoke. Don't use words, just feel the breath going in and filling your lungs then being emptied. Just watch, and soon you will come to a recognition, a great recognition that it is not simply breathing that goes in and out, it is life itself. Each breath that comes in is life infusing its energy into you. Each breath going out is a momentary death. With each breath you die and you are reborn. Each breath is a crucifixion and a resurrection.

And when you watch it, you will come to know a beautiful feeling of trust.

When you breathe out, there is no certainty that you will ever be able to breathe in again. Where is the certainty? Who has guaranteed it? Who *can* guarantee that you will be able to breathe in again? But somehow a deep trust exists; you know that you will breathe again. Otherwise breathing would become impossible. If you became so afraid—"Who knows if I let my breath out, and if I go through this small death, what is the certainty that I will be able to breathe in again? If I can't breathe in again, then it is better not to breathe out"—then you would die immediately! If you stop breathing out, you will die. But you don't do that, because a deep trust exists. That trust is part of life, is part of love. Nobody has taught it to you.

When a child starts walking for the first time, tremendous trust exists in him that he will be able to walk. Nobody has taught him. He has just seen other people walk, that's all. But how can he come to a conclusion that "I will be able to walk"? He is so tiny. People are so big, giants compared to him, and he knows that whenever he stands he falls down—but still he tries. Trust is in-built. It is in your every cell of life. The child tries, and many times he will fall; he will try again and again and again. One day, trust wins over and he starts walking.

If you watch your breath you will become aware of a deep layer of trust, a subtle trust in life—no doubt, no hesitation. If you walk, and walk with alertness, by and by you will become aware that you are not walking, you are "being walked by." It is a very subtle feeling, that life is moving through you, not that you are moving. When you feel hungry, if you are aware you will see that it is life feeling hungry within you, not you.

Becoming more alert will make you conscious of the fact that there is only one thing you have that you can call yours and that is witnessing. Everything else belongs to the universe; only witnessing belongs to you. But when you become aware of witnessing, even the idea of being "I" is dissolved. That too does not belong to you. That was part of the darkness, part of the cloudiness that had gathered around you. In the clear light, when the sky is open and the clouds have disappeared and the sun is bright, there is no possibility of any idea of being "I." Then, simply witnessing is; nothing belongs to you. That witnessing is the goal of the journey.

How to start the journey? Start becoming more and more a witness. Whatever you do, do it with deep alertness; then even small things become sacred. Then cooking or cleaning become sacred; they become worship. It is not a question of what you are doing; the question is how you are doing it. You can clean the floor like a robot, a mechanical thing; you have to clean it, so you clean it. Then you miss something beautiful. Then you waste those moments in only cleaning the floor. Cleaning the floor could have been a great experience and you missed it. The floor is clean now, but something that could have happened within you has not happened. If you had been aware, not only the floor but *you* would have felt a deep cleansing.

Clean the floor full of awareness, luminous with awareness. Work or sit or walk, but one thing has to be a continuous thread: make more and more moments of your life luminous with awareness. Let the candle of awareness burn in each moment, in each act. The cumulative effect is what enlightenment is. The cumulative effect, all the moments together, all small candles together, become a great source of light.

PART II

Love Is a Breeze

Making the Most of Romance

Don't think that love has to be permanent, and it will make your love life more beautiful because you will know that today you are together, and tomorrow perhaps you will have to part.

Love comes like a fresh, fragrant breeze into your home, fills it with freshness and fragrance, remains as long as existence allows it, and then moves out. You should not try to close all your doors, or the same fresh breeze will become absolutely stale. In life, everything is changing and change is beautiful; it gives you more and more experience, more and more awareness, more and more maturity.

NONSENSE IDEAS IN YOUR HEAD

Love is the only religion, the only god, the only mystery that has to be lived, understood. When love is understood, you have understood all the sages and all the mystics of the world. It is not anything difficult. It is as simple as your heartbeats or your breathing. It comes with you, it is not given to you by the society. And this is the point that I want to emphasize: love comes with your birth, but of course it is undeveloped as everything else is undeveloped. The child has to grow.

The society takes the advantage of the gap. The child's love will take time to grow; meanwhile the society goes on conditioning the mind of the child with ideas about love which are false. By the time you are ready to explore the world of love, you are filled with so much rubbish about love that there is not much hope for you to be able to find the authentic and discard the false.

For example, every child everywhere has been told in a thousand and one ways that love is eternal: once you love a person you love the person always. If you love a person and later on you feel that you don't love, it only means you never loved the person in the first place. Now this is a very dangerous idea. It is giving you an idea of a permanent love and in life nothing is permanent. The flowers blossom in the morning and by the evening they are gone.

Life is a continuous flux; everything is changing, moving. Nothing is static, nothing is permanent. You have been given the idea of a permanent love which is going to destroy your whole life. You will expect permanent love from the poor woman, and the woman will expect permanent love from you.

Love becomes secondary, permanence becomes primary. And love is such a delicate flower that you cannot force it to be permanent. You can have plastic flowers; that's what people have—marriage, their family, their children, their relatives, everything is plastic. Plastic has one very spiritual thing: it is permanent. Real love is as uncertain as your life is uncertain. You cannot say that you will be here tomorrow. You cannot even say that you are going to survive the next moment. Your life is continuously changing—from childhood to youth, to middle age, to old age, to death, it goes on changing.

A real love will also change.

It is possible that if you are enlightened your love has gone beyond the ordinary laws of life. It is neither changing nor permanent; it simply is. It is no more a question of how to love; you have become love itself, so whatever you do is loving. It is not that you specifically do something which is love; whatever you do, your love starts pouring through it. But before enlightenment your love is going to be the same as everything else; it will change.

If you understand that it will change, that once in a while your partner may become interested in somebody, and you have to be understanding and loving and caring and allowing her to go the way her being feels—this is a chance for you to prove to your partner that you love her. You love her; even if she is going to love somebody else, that is irrelevant. With understanding, it is possible that your love may become a lifelong affair, but remember it will not be permanent. It will have its ups and downs, it will have changes.

It is so simple to understand. When you started loving you were too young, with no experience; how can your love remain the same when you have become a mature person? Your love will also attain to some maturity. And when you have become old your love will have a different flavor to it. Love will go on changing, and once in a while love will just need an opportunity for change. In a healthy society it will be possible to take that opportunity, yet your relationship with someone will not be broken.

But it is also possible that you may have to change your lovers many times in life. There is no harm in it. In fact, by changing your lovers many times in life you will be enriched, and if the whole world follows what I am saying to you about love, the whole world will be enriched.

But a wrong idea has destroyed all possibility. The moment your partner looks at somebody, just looking, his eyes show his attraction and you freak out. You have to understand that if the man drops being interested in beautiful women on the street, beautiful actresses in the movies, that's what you want; you want him not to be interested in anything except you. But you don't understand human psychology. If he is not interested in women on the street, in the movies, why will he be interested in you? His interest in women is a guarantee that he is interested in you, that there is still a possibility that your love can go on and on.

But we are doing just the opposite. Men are trying to arrange it so that their women should not be interested in anybody other than them; they should be the woman's only focus, her total concentration. The woman is asking the same, and both are driving each other mad. Concentration on one person is bound to lead you into madness.

For a lighter life, for a more playful life, you need to be flexible. You have to remember that freedom is the highest value and if love is not giving you freedom then it is not love.

Freedom is a criterion: anything that gives you freedom is right, and anything that destroys your freedom is wrong. If you can remember this small criterion your life, slowly, will start settling on the right path about everything: your relationships, your meditations, your creativity, whatever you are.

Dropping old concepts, ugly concepts. For example in India, millions of women have died by being burned alive in the funeral pyre with their husbands. It shows that the possessiveness of the husband is so much that not only does he want to possess the woman while he is alive, he is afraid of what will happen when he is dead! He will not be able to do anything then, so it is better to take the woman with him.

And you can see that this was applied only to women—not a single man jumped into the funeral pyre of a woman in ten thousand years. What does it mean? Does it mean that only women love men and men do not love women? Does it mean that the woman has no life of her own? Only the husband's life is her life; when the husband is dead, she has to be dead?

Such nonsense ideas have settled in our heads. You have to do continuous cleaning. Whenever you see some nonsense in your head, clean it, throw it away. If you are clear and clean in the mind you will be able to find solutions for every problem that arises in your life.

?

I have recently realized that I can't even see a man, let alone love him. I have accepted my mother's angry conditioning towards men. When a man comes to me with his love, I run away, which encourages him to chase me. This game I play is so ugly. Please help me to drop this garbage, to be able to see men and to know their beauty, their gifts, their love.

If you really want to drop this garbage you have to be aware that your mother is in that garbage, and that will hurt you. You have been poisoned by your mother. Out of a hundred problems and troubles, almost 90 percent of them are because of your mothers because the child grows in the mother's womb. Even while he is in the womb, the mother's moods and emotions affect him. If the mother remains constantly angry, sad, gloomy, frustrated; if she does not want the child and the husband has forced her to have a child; if she is having the child unwillingly, all these things are going to affect the basic fabric of the child's mind. The child is in the making; it is not only the flesh and blood of the mother that influences the child, he will also be influenced by her psychology.

So while a mother is pregnant she has to be very careful because a new life is being created inside her. Anything she is going to do—fighting with the husband, fighting with the neighbors, or being frustrated for any reason—is poisoning the child's mind from the very roots. Even before he is born he is already prejudiced.

It is not only your mother who is angry with men. The vast majority of women are angry with their husbands. The same is true about husbands; most of them are angry with their wives.

But the father's anger does not affect the child so much, because the child starts inside the mother's womb, starts growing in the shadow of the mother, not in the shadow of the father. The father remains only a casual visitor. In the morning he may give the child a kiss, pat him, and go to the office. In the evening he may come and have a little talk with the child; otherwise, the whole day long the child is learning everything from the mother.

That's why every language is called the "mother tongue," because the father has no chance to speak to the child when the mother is present! Mother speaks, father listens—the child learns the language from the mother. And it is not only the language but all her attitudes.

But life as we have lived it up to now is mostly managed by men. It is a man-made society and for centuries it has had no place for women. That's why it is so strange that women are not in sympathy with other women. But their minds are also conditioned in such a way that they are sympathetic to the man.

Once in a while it also happens, as it has happened with the questioner, that deep down a woman carries her mother's feelings. The mother has been against men—and I don't see why she should not be; there is every reason. It is absolutely well founded, but it is not going to help human society or create a better future.

The past is past. You should start looking at men with fresh eyes—and particularly in this place, where our whole effort is to expose the conditioning, to dehypnotize ourselves. All the rubbish that you are carrying has to be thrown away; you have to become unburdened and light so that you can gain your own understanding, your own insight.

And the women in this community are not uneducated. You are financially capable of being independent—and as intelligent as any man. There is no need for you to be angry against men. If your mother was angry—perhaps she was not educated, perhaps she was not financially able to be independent. She wanted to fly in the open sky but she was encaged. You are not.

This is one of the reasons why I cannot communicate to the vast majority of the people of India: because the man will not be willing to listen to me; it goes against his domination, his power. And the woman cannot understand me; she is not educated. Even if she can understand me, she is not financially able to be independent; she cannot revolt against the man-made society. In most parts of India there is nothing like a women's liberation movement—not even the talk of it. No woman ever thinks that there is any possibility of liberation. She has lost all hope.

But your situation is different. You come from a country where women can receive an education, and education makes you financially able to be independent. You need not be a housewife; it is not necessary for you to be married. You can live with someone you love without any marriage.

The woman has to fight for it, the woman has to make marriage an absolutely personal affair in which the government, the state, the society, nobody has any business to interfere.

You are in a totally different space than your mother. Now, carrying her anger and her conditioning is simply stupid. Just forgive her and forget her, because if you go on having this conditioning of anger against men, you will never feel complete, because a woman or a man who is incapable of loving remains incomplete, frustrated.

As it is, it creates a vicious circle. Your anger prevents you from love, because love means dropping anger against men and moving to the diametrically opposite polarity—instead of anger, love; instead of hate, love. A quantum leap needs courage. The vicious circle is that because of your angry conditioning you cannot love men, and because you cannot love men you become more and more frustrated, and your frustration makes you more angry—this is the vicious circle. Anger brings frustration; frustration makes you more angry, more violent, more against men. That brings more anger, and the circle goes on becoming deeper and deeper. To get out of it becomes almost impossible.

You have to begin from the very beginning. The first thing is to try and understand that your mother lived in a different situation. Perhaps her anger was justified. Your situation is different, and carrying your mother within your mind is simply unreasonable. You have to live your life; you are not to live your mother's life. She suffered; now why do you want to make more suffering in the world? Why do you want to be a martyr?

Have every compassion towards your mother—I am not saying to get angry at your mother that she conditioned you. That will be again keeping you in anger, just changing the object from men to the mother. No, you need to drop the anger completely. Your mother needs your compassion; she must have suffered, and that created anger in her. But *you* are not suffering. You can put your anger aside and you have a fresh look at men. If their forefathers have caused women to suffer it is beyond their power to undo it. What has happened, has happened. Now they can feel a deep apology in their hearts for what man has done to women. These types of men are a different category of people.

I am trying to create every possibility for the emergence of a new kind of human being who is not contaminated by the past, who is discontinuous with the past. It is a difficult job; it is almost like hitting my head against the wall. But I am determined to go on hitting—I trust in my head! And the wall is very old and ancient. It may hurt me, but it has to fall some day; its time is finished. It has already lived more than its life span.

So meditate more, and be aware when your mother's voice starts speaking to your mind. Slowly, slowly put that voice to sleep. Don't listen to it; it will spoil your whole life. You have to learn how to love. And when he is loved, the man becomes more polite, nicer, a gentleman. He loses his corners, becomes softer. Through love, the woman starts blossoming; otherwise she remains a closed bud. Only in love, when the sun of love rises, she opens her petals. Only in love her eyes start having a different depth, a different shine; her face starts having a joyous outlook. She has a deep transformation through love; she comes to maturity, of age.

So get rid of the conditioning that your mother unconsciously has given to you. You have accepted it unconsciously. The way to get rid of it is to become conscious of it. It is a good beginning that you have asked. This is the beginning of consciousness—just the very ABC. You have to go far to change your mind completely, to be fresh, unconditioned, open and vulnerable.

And because of this conditioning you have been playing this ugly game, that whenever a man comes to you with his love, you run away, which naturally encourages him to chase you. That you enjoy, that he is chasing you. Every woman enjoys that. It *is* ugly, and you are not aware of its deeper implications. It means you are the prey; the man is the hunter and he is chasing game. You are allowing supremacy to the man, unknowingly. It has been traditionally given to you that the initiative in love should be taken by men, not by women; it is against a woman's grace. Those are all rotten ideas—why be number two from the very beginning? If you love a man, why wait? I know many women who have waited for years because they wanted the man to take the initiative. But they have fallen in love with such men who were not going to take the initiative.

I know one woman in Bombay who was in love with J. Krishnamurti. Her whole life she remained unmarried, waiting for J. Krishnamurti to take the initiative. She is one of the most beautiful women but J. Krishnamurti is utterly fulfilled within himself, he does not need anybody else to complete him. Obviously, he never took any initiative. And the woman, out of the conditioning of thousands of years, of course could not take the initiative; that is against feminine grace, that is "primitive."

There is really no reason for the woman to wait for the man to take the initiative. If a woman feels love for someone, she should take the initiative and she should not feel humiliated if the man is not willing. This will give them equality. These are small things that will make the liberation of women possible.

But the woman has been always trying to be "game." She attracts the man, she tries in every way to attract him by her beauty, by her clothes, her perfume, her hairdo—all that she can manage. She attracts the man, and once the man is attracted, then she starts running away. But she does not run too fast, either. She goes on looking back, to see whether that fellow is coming or not. If he is left far behind, she waits. When he comes close again she starts running.

This is stupid; love should be a clean affair. You love someone, you express your love and tell the other person, "You are not obliged to say yes; your no will be perfectly respected. It is just my desire. You need not unwillingly say yes to me, because that yes is dangerous unless you also feel love for me. Only then can our life become a completion."

A woman and a man in love can move into meditation very easily. Meditation and love are such close phenomena that if you move into meditation, your love energies start overflowing. If you really fall in love with someone who loves you, your meditative energies start growing; they are very deeply joined experiences. Hence I am in favor of both.

?

I have heard you speak about the ego and how, with awareness, one can see that it does not exist. But I realize that I never put much emphasis on awareness. Can you please show the way to become more aware?

Love is enough unto itself, if your love is not the ordinary, biological instinctive love. If it is not part of your ego, if it is not a power trip to dominate someone—if your love is just a pure joy, rejoicing in the being of the other for no reason at all, a sheer joy—awareness will follow this pure love just like a shadow. You need not worry about awareness.

There are only two ways: either you become aware, then love follows as a shadow; or you become so loving that awareness comes of its own accord. They are two sides of the same coin. You need not bother about the other side; just keep hold of one side and the other side cannot escape! The other side is bound to come.

And the path of love is easier, rosier, innocent, simple.

The path of awareness is a little arduous. Those who cannot love, for them I suggest the path of awareness. There are people who cannot love—their hearts have become stones. Their upbringing, their culture, their society has killed the very capacity to love because this whole world is not run by love, it is run by cunningness. To succeed in this world you don't need love, you need a hard heart and a sharp mind. In fact, you don't need the heart at all.

In this world, the people of the heart are crushed, exploited, oppressed. This world is run by the cunning, by the clever, by the heartless, and the cruel. So the whole society is managed in such a way that every child starts losing his heart, and his energy starts moving directly towards the head. The heart is ignored.

I have heard an ancient parable from Tibet, that in the beginning of time the heart used to be exactly in the middle part of the body. But because of continuously being pushed aside, out of the way, now it is no longer in the middle of the body. Now the poor fellow waits by the side of the road—"If some day you need me, I am here"—but it gets no nourishment, no encouragement. Instead it gets all kinds of condemnation.

If you do something and you say, "I did it because I felt like doing it," everybody is going to laugh: "Felt? Have you lost your head? Give your reason, your logic for doing it. Feeling is not a reason to do anything."

Even if you fall in love, you have to find reasons why you have fallen in love: because the woman's nose is beautiful, her eyes have such depth, her body is so proportionate. These are not the reasons. You have never added up all these reasons on your calculator and then found that this woman seems to be worthy of falling in love with: "Fall in love with this woman—exactly the right length of nose, the right kind of hair, the right color, the right proportion of the body. What more do you want?"

But this is not the way that anybody ever falls in love. You fall in love. Then just to satisfy the idiots around you that you are not a fool, you have calculated everything and only then you have taken the step. It is a reasonable, rational, logical step.

Nobody hears the heart.

And the mind is so chattering, so continuously chattering—yakkety-yak, yakkety-yak—that even if the heart sometimes says something, it never reaches to you. It cannot reach. The bazaar in your head is buzzing so much that it is impossible, absolutely impossible for the heart. Slowly, the heart stops saying anything. Not heard again and again, ignored again and again, it falls silent.

The head runs the show in the society; otherwise, we would have lived in a totally different world—more loving, less hate, less war, no possibility of nuclear weapons. The heart will never give support for any destructive technology to be developed. The heart will never be in the service of death. It is life: it throbs for life, it beats for life.

Because of the whole conditioning of the society, the method of awareness has to be chosen, because awareness appears to be very logical and rational. But if you can love, then there is no need to go on a long, arduous route unnecessarily. Love is the shortest way, the most natural—so easy that it is possible even for a small child. It needs no training. You are born with the quality of it, if it is not corrupted by others.

But love should be pure. It should not be impure.

You will be surprised to know that the English word "love" comes from a very ugly root in Sanskrit. It comes from *lobh. Lobh* means "greed."

And as far as ordinary love is concerned, it is a kind of greed. That's why there are people who love money, who love houses; there are people who love this, who love that. Even if they love a woman or a man, it is simply their greed; they want to possess everything beautiful. It is a power trip. Hence, you will find lovers continuously fighting, fighting about such trivia that they both feel ashamed "about what things we go on fighting!" In their silent moments when they are alone, they wonder, "Do I become possessed by some evil spirit? Such trivia, so meaningless!" But it is not a question of trivia; it is a question of who has power, who is more dominant, whose voice is heard.

Love cannot exist in such circumstances.

I have heard a story: In the life of one of the great emperors of India, Akbar, there is a small story. He was very much interested in all kinds of talented people, and from all over India he had collected nine people, the most talented geniuses, who were known as the "nine jewels of Akbar's court."

One day, just gossiping with his vice-councillors, he said, "Last night I was discussing with my wife. She is very insistent that every husband is henpecked. I tried hard, but she says, 'I know many families, but I have never found any husband who is not henpecked.' What do you think?" he asked the councillors.

One of the councillors, Birbal, said, "Perhaps she is right, because you could not prove it. You yourself are a henpecked husband; otherwise, you could have given her a good beating, then and there proving that you are the husband and you are in charge."

Akbar said, "That I cannot do, because I have to live with her. It is easy to advise somebody else to beat his wife. Can you beat your wife?"

Birbal said, "No, I cannot. I simply accept that I am a henpecked husband, and your wife is right."

But Akbar said, "It has to be proved, one way or another. Surely in the capital there must be at least one husband who is not henpecked. There is no rule in the world that has no exception, and this is not a scientific rule at all." He said to Birbal, "You take my two beautiful Arabian horses"—one was black, one was white—"and go around the capital. If you can find a man who is not henpecked, you can give him the choice: whichever horse he wants is a present from me." They were valuable. In those days horses were very valuable, and these were the most beautiful horses.

Birbal said, "It is useless, but if you say so I will go."

He went, and everybody was found to be henpecked. It was so easy to see! Birbal would just call the person and his wife to their front door and ask the husband, "Are you henpecked or not?"

The man would look at his wife and say, "You should have asked when I was alone. This is not right, it will create unnecessary trouble. Just for a horse I am not going to destroy my life. You take your horses, I don't want either one of them."

But then he came upon one man who was sitting in front of his house, with two persons massaging him. He was a champion wrestler, a very strong man. Birbal thought, "Perhaps this man—he could kill anybody, even without any weapons. If he just got hold of your neck you would be finished!" Birbal said, "Can I ask you a question?"

The man stood up and said, "Question? What question?"

Birbal asked him, "Are you henpecked?"

That man said, "First, let us greet each other, a handshake." He crushed Birbal's hand and said, "I will not let go of your hand until tears start coming from your eyes! You dare to ask me such a question?"

Birbal was nearly dying—he himself was almost a man of steel, but tears started coming, and he said, "Just let go of me! You are not henpecked! Clearly I have just come to the wrong place to ask such a thing. But where is your wife?"

The man pointed and said, "Look, she is there, cooking my breakfast." A very small woman was cooking his breakfast.

The woman was so small and the man was so big that Birbal thought there really was a possibility that perhaps this man was not henpecked. He could kill this woman! So he said, "Now there is no need to go any further into investigation. You can choose either horse from these two, black and white, as a reward from the king for the man who is not henpecked."

And just at that moment, that small woman said, "Don't choose the black! Choose the white, or I will make your life a hell!"

The man said, "No, no, I was anyway going to choose the white. You just keep quiet."

And Birbal said, "You get neither white nor black. It is all finished, you lost the game. Even you are a henpecked husband."

There is a continuous fight for domination. Love cannot blossom in such an atmosphere. The man is fighting in the world for all kinds of ambitions. The woman is fighting the man because she is afraid: he is out of the house the whole day. "Who knows? He may be having affairs with other women." She is jealous, suspicious; she wants to be sure that this man remains controlled. So in the house the man is fighting with the wife, in the outside he is fighting with the world. Where do you think the flower of love can blossom?

The flower of love can blossom only when there is no ego, when there is no effort to dominate, when one is humble, when one is trying not to be somebody but is ready to be nobody. Then awareness will come of its own accord, and this is the most beautiful way, the most innocent way: a path full of flowers, a path that passes through beautiful lakes, rivers, groves, greenery.

If you can easily be heartful, forget all about awareness; it will come of its own accord. Each step of love will bring its own awareness. This love will not be falling in love; I call it rising in love.

? **How is it possible for a woman to be in love and still centered in herself and in her own individuality?**

The question has many implications.

First, you do not understand what being centered means. Second, you also have no experience of the phenomenon of love. I can say this with absolute authority, because your question supplies all the evidence for what I am saying.

Love and centering are one phenomenon, they are not two. If you have known love, you cannot be anything but centered.

Love means coming to be at ease with existence. It may be through a lover, it may be through a friend, or it may be simply direct and immediate—through the sunrise, the sunset. The very experience of love will make you centered. This has been the whole philosophy of devotees down through the ages. Love is their science; centering is the result.

But there are people—and there are only two kinds of people—who have a dominant reasoning, logic. Their heart is undeveloped. And there are people whose heart is blossoming and now reason, rationality only function as servants to the heart. Man's misery is that he is trying to do the impossible: he is trying to force the heart to serve the mind, which is impossible. This is your chaos, this is your mess.

The question has arisen out of the ordinary experience called love. It is not love, it is only called love—just a glimpse, just a small taste, which is not going to be a nourishment. On the contrary, it is going to become a pathological state because one moment you are high and everything is just far out, and the next moment all is dark, you cannot believe that there has been anything significant in your life. All those moments of love appear to have happened in dreams, or perhaps you have imagined them. And these dark moments are absolutely joined with the beautiful moments.

This is the dialectic of human mind. It functions through opposites. You will love a man and you will love the man for absolutely wrong reasons. You will love the man or the woman because you are carrying within you an image of the other. The boy has got it from the mother and the girl has got it from the father. All lovers are searching for their mothers, their fathers—in the final analysis they are all searching for the womb and its beautiful, relaxed state.

Psychologically, the eternal quest for *moksha*, ultimate liberation, enlightenment, can be reduced to the basic psychological fact that man has already known the most beautiful, the most peaceful state before he was born. Now, if something greater does not happen in his life, some exposure to the divine, to the universal, he is going to remain miserable because—unconsciously—every moment there is judgment.

He knows he has lived for nine months and, remember, for a child in the mother's womb, nine months are almost eternity because he does not know how to count, he does not have any clock. Each moment is enough unto itself. He does not know there is going to be another moment afterwards, so each moment is a surprise. And with no worry, with no tension about food, about clothes, about shelter, he is absolutely at ease, relaxed, centered. There is nothing to distract him from the center.

There is nobody there even to say hello.

This experience of nine months of being centered, of immense joy, peace, aloneness . . . the other is no more there; you are the world, you are the whole. Nothing is missing, everything is supplied by nature without any effort on your part. But life confronts you in a totally different way—antagonistically, competitively. Everybody is your enemy, because everybody is in the same market; everybody is your enemy because everybody has the same desires, the same ambition. You are bound to come into conflict with millions of people.

It is because of this inner antagonism that all the cultures of the world have created a certain system of etiquette, familiarity, formality, and they have emphasized it continuously to the child: "You have to respect your father." All the cultures all over the world throughout the whole of history, why are they all insisting to the child, "You should respect your father"? There is some suspicion that if he is left alone, the child is not going to respect the father; that much is certain, simple logic. In fact, the child is going to hate. Every girl hates her mother.

To hide it—because it will be very difficult to live in a society where all your wounds are uncovered and everybody is walking around with uncovered wounds—a certain ethos, a morality, a certain style of life has to cover it, and to show just the opposite, that you love your mother, that you love and respect your father. Deep down just the opposite is the case.

You have been divided into two parts by the society. The false part has been given all respect, because the false is created by the society. The real is denied any respectability, because the real comes from nature, which is beyond the control of any society, culture, or civilization. Each child has to be trained in lies, has to be programmed in such a way that he will be subservient to the society, a docile slave.

All societies are breaking the very spine of every child so he becomes spineless. He cannot raise his voice, he cannot question anything. His life is just not his own. He loves, but his love is false. From the very beginning he was told to love his mother "because she is your mother"—as if being a mother has some intrinsic quality or some obligation that you should love her. But it has been accepted that the mother should be loved.

My emphasis is that the mother should be loving, and no child should ever be told to love somebody unless it happens on its own. Yes, the mother, the father, the family can create a milieu without saying anything; the whole energy can generate, can trigger your own forces of love.

But never say to anybody that love is a duty. It is not. Duty is a false substitute for love. When you cannot love, society goes on supplying duties. They may appear to be love, but inside there is nothing loving in it; on the contrary, it is only social formality. And you become so accustomed to social formalities that you forget completely that there are things which are waiting to happen in your life but you are so occupied that you don't give space, you don't allow love to blossom in you.

Hence, you don't know that centering and love are one thing.

Centering is more appealing to the intellectual. Nothing has to be believed; there is nobody else to whom you have to surrender.

It is because of the other that every love affair becomes a tragedy.

In Indian literature there are no tragedies. In my student days I was asking my professors, "Why are tragedies missing in Indian literature?" And not a single teacher or professor was able to say something significant about it.

They simply shrugged their shoulders and they said, "You are strange; you find such questions. I have been in this university for thirty years and nobody has asked."

I said, "To me it seems very obvious that the question has deep roots in the culture." In all other countries except India there are tragedies—beautiful stories, novels, fiction—but in India they are missing. And the reason is India is a more ancient land than any other land. It has learned many things from experience, and one of them is that which should not be, should not be talked about; hence, there should be no tragedy.

Their logic can be understood. If man feels that life is everywhere a comedy, then there is a possibility he might continue deceiving himself. He might never tell anybody his problems because he thinks nobody has problems. Why become a laughingstock? Something is wrong with you, just keep quiet. There is no point in exposing yourself to a cruel society that will simply laugh at you and prove that you are an idiot and you don't know how to live.

But it is not so simple. It is not a question just of knowing how to live. It is a question first of dropping all that is false in you. The false comes from the outside. And when all that is false is dropped and you are utterly naked before existence, the real will start growing in you. This is the situation which has to be fulfilled for the real to grow, to blossom, and to bring you to the ultimate meaning and truth of life.

It has to be remembered: You can start either from centering—the moment you are centered you will suddenly find immense love overflowing—or you can start from love. And the moment your love is without any jealousy, without any conditionings, but just a sharing of the dance of the heart, you will experience centering.

They are two sides of the same coin. Centering is a more intellectual, scientific method. Love has a different source in you—your heart. It is more poetic, it is more aesthetic, it is more sensitive, it is more feminine, it is more beautiful. And it is easier than centering.

My suggestion is, first drop all false ideas about love. Let something real grow in you, and centering will be coming, enlightenment will be coming. But if you find it very difficult to start with love, then don't feel despair. You can move directly through centering. You can call it meditation, you can call it awareness. But in each case, the ultimate result is the same: you are centered and overflowing with love.

"LOVE HURTS" AND OTHER MISUNDERSTANDINGS

Love never hurts anybody. And if you feel you have been hurt by love, it is something else in you, not your loving quality, that feels hurt. Unless you see this you will go on moving in the same circles again and again. What you call love can hide many unloving things in you; the human mind has been very clever, cunning, in deceiving others and in deceiving itself, too. The mind puts beautiful labels on ugly things, it tries to cover your wounds with flowers. This is one of the first things you have to go into, if you want to understand what love is.

"Love" as people ordinarily use the word is not love; it is lust. And lust is bound to cause hurt, because to desire somebody as an object is to offend that person. It is an insult, it is violent. When you move with lust toward somebody, how long can you pretend it is love? Something that is superficial will look like love, but scratch a little bit and hidden behind it is sheer lust. Lust is animalistic. To look at anybody with lust is to insult, humiliate, is to reduce the other person to a thing, to a commodity. No person ever likes to be used; that's the most ugly thing you can do to anybody. No person is a commodity, no person is a means toward any end.

This is the difference between lust and love. Lust uses the other person to fulfill some of your desires. The other is only used, and when the use is complete you can throw the other person away. It has no more use to you; its function is fulfilled. This is the most immoral act in existence, using the other as a means.

Love is just the opposite of it: respecting the other as an end unto himself or herself. When you love someone as an end unto himself, then there is no feeling of hurt; you become enriched through it. Love makes everybody rich.

Secondly, love can only be true if there is no ego hiding behind it; otherwise love becomes only an ego trip. It is a subtle way to dominate. And one has to be very conscious because this desire to dominate is very deep-rooted. It never comes naked; it always comes hidden beneath beautiful garments, decorated.

Parents never say that their children are their possessions, they never say that they want to dominate the children, but that's actually what they do. They say they want to help, they say they want them to be intelligent, to be healthy, to be blissful, but—and that "but" is a great but—it has to be according to their ideas. Even their children's happiness has to be decided by the parents' ideas; the children have to be happy according to the parents' expectations.

Children have to be intelligent, but at the same time obedient, too. This is asking for the impossible! The intelligent person cannot be obedient; the obedient person has to lose some of his intelligence. Intelligence can say yes only when it feels deep agreement with you. It cannot say yes just because you are bigger, more powerful, authoritative—a father, a mother, a priest, a politician. It cannot say yes just because of the authority that you carry with you. Intelligence is rebellious, and no parents would like their children to be rebellious. Rebellion will be against their hidden desire to dominate.

Husbands say they love their wives, but it is just domination. They are so jealous, so possessive, how can they be loving? Wives go on saying they love their husbands, but twenty-four hours a day they are creating hell; in every possible way they are reducing the husband to something ugly. The henpecked husband is an ugly phenomenon. And the problem is that first the wife reduces the husband to a henpecked husband and then she loses interest in him, because who can remain interested in a henpecked husband? He seems to be worthless; he does not seem to be man enough.

First the husband tries to make the wife just his possession, and once she is a possession he loses interest. There is some hidden logic in it: his whole interest was to possess; now that is finished, and he would like to try some other woman so he can again go on another trip of possession.

Beware of these ego numbers. Then you will be hurt, because the person you are trying to possess is bound to revolt in some way or other, is bound to sabotage your tricks, your strategies because nobody loves anything more than freedom. Even love is secondary to freedom; freedom is the highest value. Love can be sacrificed for freedom, but freedom cannot be sacrificed for love. And that's what we have been doing for centuries, sacrificing freedom for love. Then there is antagonism, conflict, and every opportunity is used to hurt each other.

Love in its purest form is a sharing of joy. It asks nothing in return, it expects nothing; hence how can you feel hurt? When you don't expect, there is no possibility of being hurt. Then whatsoever comes is good, and if nothing comes, that too is good. Your joy was to give, not to get. Then one can love from thousands of miles away; there is no need even to be physically present.

Love is a spiritual phenomenon; lust is physical. Ego is psychological; love is spiritual. You will have to learn the very alphabet of love. You will have to start from the very beginning, from scratch; otherwise you will be hurt again and again. And remember, only you can help yourself; nobody else is responsible.

How can anybody help you? Nobody else can destroy your ego. If you cling to it, nobody can destroy it; if you have invested in it, nobody can destroy it. I can only share my understanding with you. The buddhas can only show the way; then you have to go, then you have to follow the way. Nobody can lead you, holding your hand.

That's what you would like: you would like to play the game of being dependent. And remember, the person who plays the game of being dependent will take revenge. Soon he would like in some way for the other to be dependent on him or on her. If the wife is dependent on the husband for money, then she will try to make the husband dependent on her for other things. It is a mutual arrangement. They both become crippled, they both become paralyzed; they cannot exist without each other. Even the idea that the husband was happy without the wife hurts her, that he was laughing with the guys in the club hurts her. She is not interested in his happiness; in fact she cannot believe it: "How did he dare to be happy without me? He has to depend on me!"

The husband does not feel good that the wife was laughing with somebody, was enjoying, was cheerful. He wants all her cheerfulness to be totally possessed by him; it is his property. The dependent person will make you dependent also.

Fear is never love, and love is never afraid. There is nothing to lose for love. Why should love be afraid? Love only gives. It is not a business transaction, so there is no question of loss or profit. Love enjoys giving, just as flowers enjoy releasing their fragrance. Why should they be afraid? Why should you be afraid?

Remember, fear and love never exist together; they cannot. No coexistence is possible. Fear is just the opposite of love.

People ordinarily think hate is the opposite of love. That is wrong, absolutely wrong. Fear is the opposite of love. Hate is love standing on its head; it is a headstand but it is not opposite to love. The person who hates simply shows that somewhere, he still loves. The love has gone sour, but it is still there. Fear is the real opposite. Fear means that now the whole love energy has disappeared.

Love is outgoing, fearlessly reaching to the other, tremendously trusting that it will be received—and it is always received. Fear is shrinking within yourself, closing yourself, closing all the doors, all the windows so that no sun, no wind, no rain can reach you, you are so afraid. You are entering into your grave alive.

Fear is a grave, love is a temple. In love, life comes to its ultimate peak. In fear, life falls to the level of death. Fear stinks, love is fragrant. Why should you be afraid?

Be afraid of your ego, be afraid of your lust, be afraid of your greed, be afraid of your possessiveness; be afraid of your jealousy—but there is no question of being afraid of love. Love is divine! Love is like light. When there is light, darkness cannot exist. When there is love, fear cannot exist.

Love can make a great celebration out of your life, but only love—not lust, not ego, not possessiveness, not jealousy, not dependence.

?

I think I understand what you mean when you say it is not love that hurts. Nevertheless, the kind of love you are talking about is not so easy to find. So the process of

learning and growing into a more mature love is often very painful. Is pain just an inevitable part of growth?

Growth is painful because you have been avoiding a thousand and one pains in your life. By avoiding them you cannot destroy them, they go on accumulating. You go on swallowing your pains and they remain in your system. That's why growth is painful: when you start growing, when you decide to grow, you have to face all the pains that you have repressed. You cannot just bypass them.

You have been brought up in a wrong way. Unfortunately, until now, not a single society has existed on the earth which has not been repressive of pain. All societies depend on repression. Two things they repress: one is pain, another is pleasure. And they repress pleasure also because of pain. Their reasoning is that if you are not too happy you will never become too unhappy; if great joy is destroyed you will never be in deep pain. To avoid pain, they avoid pleasure. To avoid death, they avoid life.

And the logic has something in it. Both grow together; if you want to have a life of ecstasy you will have to accept many agonies. If you want the peaks of the Himalayas then you will also have the valleys. But nothing is wrong with the valleys; your approach just has to be different. You can enjoy both—the peak is beautiful, so is the valley. And there are moments when one should enjoy the peak and there are moments when one should relax in the valley.

The peak is sunlit, it is in a dialogue with the sky. The valley is dark, but whenever you want to relax you have to move into the darkness of the valley. If you want to have peaks you will need to grow roots into the valley: the deeper your roots go, the higher your tree will grow. The tree cannot grow without roots and the roots have to move deep into the soil.

Pain and pleasure are intrinsic parts of life. People are so much afraid of pain that they repress it, they avoid any situation that brings pain, they go on dodging pain. And finally they stumble upon the fact that if you really want to avoid pain you will have to avoid pleasure, too. That's why your monks avoid pleasure—they are afraid of it. In fact they are simply avoiding all possibilities of pain. They know that if you avoid pleasure then naturally great pain is not possible; it comes only as a shadow of pleasure. Then you walk on the plain ground; you never move on the peaks and you never fall into the valleys. But then you are part of the living dead, then you are not alive.

Life exists between this polarity. This tension between pain and pleasure makes you capable of creating great music; music exists only in this tension. Destroy the polarity and you will be dull, you will be stale, you will be dusty. You won't have any meaning and you will never know what splendor is. You will have missed life. One who wants to know life and live life has to accept and embrace death. They come together, they are two aspects of a single phenomenon.

That's why growth is painful. You have to go into all those pains that you have been avoiding. It hurts. You have to go through all those wounds that somehow you have managed not to look at. But the deeper you go into pain, the deeper is your capacity to go into pleasure. If you can go into pain to the uttermost limit, you will be able to touch heaven.

I have heard that a seeker came to a Zen master and asked, "How shall we avoid heat and cold?"

Metaphorically, he is asking, "How should we avoid pleasure and pain?" That is the Zen way of talking about pleasure and pain, "heat and cold."

"How shall we avoid heat and cold?"

The master answered, "Be hot, be cold."

To be free of pain the pain has to be accepted, inevitably and naturally. Pain is pain—a simple, painful fact. *Suffering*, however, is only and always the refusal of pain, the claim that life should not be painful. It is the rejection of a fact, the denial of life and of the nature of things. Death is the mind that minds dying. Where there is no fear of death, who is there to die?

Man is unique among creatures in his knowledge of death and in his laughter. The miracle is that then, he can even create out of death something new: he can die laughing! And if you can die laughing, only then will you give a valid proof that you must have lived laughing. Death is the final statement of your whole life—the conclusion, the concluding remark. How you have lived will be shown by your death, how you die.

Can you die laughing? Then you were a grown-up person. If you die crying, weeping, clinging, then you were a child. You were not grown up, you were immature. If you die crying, weeping, clinging to life, that simply shows you have been avoiding death and you have been avoiding life too, with all its pains.

Growth is facing the reality, encountering the fact, whatever it is. And let me repeat: pain is simply pain; there is no suffering in it. Suffering comes from your desire that the pain should not be there, that there is something wrong in pain. Watch, witness, and you will be surprised. You have a headache: the pain is there but suffering is not there. Suffering is a secondary phenomenon, pain is primary. The headache is there, the pain is there; it is simply a fact. There is no judgment about it. You don't call it good or bad, you don't give it any value; it is just a fact.

The rose is a fact, so is the thorn. The day is a fact, so is the night. The head is a fact, so is the headache. You simply take note of it.

Buddha taught his disciples that when you have a headache simply say twice, "Headache, headache." Take note, but don't evaluate, don't say, "Why? Why has this headache happened to me? It should not happen to me." The moment you say, "It should not" you bring suffering in. Now suffering is created by you, not by the headache. Suffering is your antagonistic interpretation, suffering is your denial of the fact.

And the moment you say, "It should not be" you have started avoiding it, you have started turning yourself away from it. You would like to be occupied in something so that you can forget it. You turn the radio or the television on, or you go to the club, or you start reading. You divert yourself, you distract yourself. Now that pain has not been witnessed; you have simply distracted yourself. That pain will be absorbed by your system.

Let this key be very deeply understood: if you can witness your headache without taking any antagonistic attitude, without avoiding it, without escaping from it; if you can just be there, meditatively there—"Headache, headache"—if you can just simply see it, the headache will go in its time. I am not saying that it will go miraculously, that just by your seeing it will go. It will go in its time. But it will not be absorbed by your system, it will not poison your system. It will be there, you will take note of it, and it will be gone. It will be released.

When you witness a certain thing in yourself, it cannot enter into your system. It always enters when you avoid it, when you escape from it. When you are absent, then it enters into your system. Only when you are absent can a pain become part of your being—if you are present, your very presence prevents it from becoming part of your being.

And if you can go on taking note of your pains you will not be accumulating them. You have not been taught the right clue, so you go on avoiding. Then you accumulate so much pain, you are afraid to face it, you are afraid to accept it. Growth becomes painful; it is because of wrong conditioning. Otherwise growth is not painful, growth is utterly pleasant.

When the tree grows and becomes bigger do you think there is pain? There is no pain. Even when a child is born, if the mother accepts it there will be no pain. But the mother rejects it; the mother is afraid. She becomes tense, she tries to hold the child inside, which is not possible. The child is ready to go out into the world, the child is ready to leave the mother. He is ripe, the womb cannot contain him anymore. If the womb contains him any longer the mother will die and the child will die. But the mother is afraid. She has heard that it is very painful to give birth to a child—birth pangs, birth pain—she is afraid. And out of fear she becomes tense and closed.

For others—and in primitive societies those people still exist—childbirth is so simple, with no pain at all. On the contrary, you will be surprised, the greatest ecstasy happens to the woman in childbirth—not pain, not agony at all, but the greatest ecstasy. No sexual orgasm is so satisfying and so tremendous as the orgasm that happens to the woman when she gives birth to a child naturally. The whole sexual mechanism of the woman pulsates as it cannot pulsate in any lovemaking. The child is coming from the deepest core of the woman. No man can ever penetrate a woman to that core. And the pulsation arises from the inside. The pulsation is a must; that pulsation will come like waves, great tidal waves of joy. Only that will help the child to come out, only that will help the passage to open for the child. So there will be great pulsation and the whole sexual being of the woman will have tremendous joy.

But what actually has happened to humanity is just the opposite: the woman comes to feel the greatest agony of her life. And this is a mind creation, this is wrong upbringing. The physical birth can be natural if you accept it, and so it is with your birth as a loving being. Growth means you are being born every day. Birth does not end the day you were born; on that day it simply starts, it is only a beginning. The day you left the womb of your mother you were not born, you just *started* being born; that was just the beginning. And a person goes on being born till he dies. It is not that you are born in a single moment. Your birth process continues for seventy, eighty, ninety years, however long you live. It is a continuum.

And every day you will feel joy: growing new leaves, new foliage, new flowers, new branches, rising higher and higher and touching new altitudes. You will be getting deeper, higher; you will be reaching to peaks. Growth will not be painful.

But growth is painful—it is because of you, your wrong conditioning. You have been taught not to grow; you have been taught to remain static, you have been taught to cling to the familiar and the known. That's why each time the known disappears from your hands you start crying. A toy has been broken, a pacifier has been taken away.

Remember, only one thing is going to help you, and that is awareness—nothing else. Growth will remain painful if you don't accept life and love in all its ups and downs. The summer has to be accepted and the winter, too.

This is what I call meditation. Meditation is when you are emptied of all that is old and told and done to death. Then you see. Or rather, then there is *seeing*, the birth of the new. But you will have to go through many pains, many agonies. It is because you have lived in a certain society, in a certain culture—Hindu, Mohammedan, Christian, Indian, German, Japanese. These are different ways of avoiding pain and nothing else. You have been part of a culture, that's why growth is painful, because the culture tries to make you not grow; it wants you to remain juvenile. It does not allow you to move psychologically as you move physiologically.

In the First World War and then again in the Second World War, psychologists became aware of a very strange fact: that man's average mental age is not more than twelve or thirteen. Even the man who is seventy, his mental age is somewhere between ten and thirteen. What does it mean? It simply means he stopped growing at ten; the body continued but the mind stopped. No society allows grown-up minds. Why? Because grown-up minds are dangerous for the social structure; they are rebellious. They are dangerous for the social structure because they will see all the kinds of stupidities that go on in the name of culture, society, nation.

Now see: the earth is one, and man still remains divided. All the problems of humanity can be solved if nations disappear. There is no problem, actually there is no problem; the basic problem is created by the boundaries of nations. Now the technology exists that can feed all the people of the world, there is no need for any starvation. But that is not possible, because those boundaries won't allow it.

A grown-up person will be able to see all this nonsense, a grown-up person will be able to see it through and through. A grown-up person cannot be reduced to a slave.

Take hold of your being. Face your pains and throw off all kinds of bondages, because only by being free of all bondages will you be able to sing your song and dance your dance.

In spring, hundreds of flowers; in autumn, a harvest moon.
In summer, a refreshing breeze; in winter, snow.
If useless things do not hang in your mind,
Any season is a good season.

It is a Zen saying. "If useless things don't hang in your mind . . ." Growth is painful because you are carrying so many useless things in your mind. You should have dropped them long before. But you have not been taught to drop anything, you have only been taught to hold on to everything—meaningful, meaningless. Because you are carrying so many hang-ups, growth is difficult. Otherwise growth will be so smooth, just like a bud opens into a flower.

? **My girlfriend told me I am a little boring, very dependent, and a victim. Then I felt guilty and depressed and utterly unworthy.**

I began to feel inside me a big no: towards existence, life, love. Meanwhile I observed in me this destructive energy and I felt that I somehow enjoyed it! Is it possible to use this energy in some creative way?

Your question is an example of the stupid conclusions that mind comes to. Perhaps you may not have looked into it and its contradictions. I would like to go into the very psychology of such questions. They are not only within you, they are within many. You are courageous to expose yourself.

The exposure begins, "My girlfriend told me I am a little boring." Your girlfriend is very compassionate, because each man finally becomes *very* boring, not "a little" boring. Do you realize the fact that what you call love is a repetition, the same stupid gymnastics again and again? And in this whole stupid game the man is the loser. He is dissipating his energy, perspiring, huffing, puffing, and the girl keeps her eyes closed, thinking, "It is a question only of two or three minutes and this nightmare will be finished."

People are so noninventive, they take it for granted that going through the same act again and again is making them more interesting. That's why I say your girlfriend is very compassionate; she only told you that you are a *little* boring. I say to you, you are utterly boring.

When the Christian missionaries came to the East, the Eastern people discovered that they knew only one posture of making love: the woman underneath and those ugly beasts on top of the delicate woman. That's where it got the name "the missionary position."

India is an ancient land and the birthplace of many sciences, particularly sexology. A book of tremendous importance, by Vatsyayana, has been in existence for five thousand years. The name of the book is *Kama Sutra*, hints for making love. And it comes from a man of deep meditation—he has created eighty-four positions for lovemaking. Naturally the positions should change; otherwise you are bound to be boring. Vatsyayana recognizes the fact that the same lovemaking position creates boredom, a feeling of utter stupidity, because you are always doing the same thing. He invented eighty-four postures to make the love lives of couples a little interesting. Nobody in the whole world has written a book of the caliber of *Kama Sutra*. But it could only have come from a man of immense clarity, of deep meditativeness.

What is your lovemaking? If you look at your lovemaking, you yourself will feel that it is all boring. And particularly for the woman it is more boring, because the man is finished in two or three minutes and the woman has not even started. And all around the world, cultures have enforced in the minds of women that they are not supposed even to enjoy or move or be playful—that is called "dirty"; prostitutes do it, not ladies. Ladies have to lie down almost dead and let that old guy do whatsoever he wants to do. So it is nothing new, there is nothing new even to see.

You should not take it as a personal insult. Your girlfriend is telling you something really sincere and honest. Have you given her orgasmic joy? Or have you only used her to throw out your sexual energy? Have you reduced her into a commodity? She has been conditioned to accept it, but this mere "acceptance" cannot be joyful.

You make love on the same bed where you fight every day. In fact fighting is the preface: throwing pillows, shouting at each other, arguing about everything, and then, feeling tired, some negotiation is needed. Your love is only a negotiation. If you are a man of aesthetic sensibility, your love chamber should be a sacred place, because it is in that love chamber that life is born. It should have beautiful flowers, incense, fragrance; you should enter into it with deep respect.

And love should not be just an abrupt thing where you just grab the woman. This hit-and-run affair is not love. Love should have a preface of beautiful music, of dancing together, of meditating together. And it should not be a mind thing, that the whole time you are thinking of how to get her to make love and then go to sleep. It should be a deeper involvement of your whole being, not projected by the mind but coming spontaneously. Beautiful music, fragrance, you are dancing hand in hand, you have again become small children playing with flowers. If spontaneously, lovemaking happens in this sacred atmosphere it will have a different quality.

You should understand that the woman is capable of multiple orgasms, because she does not lose any energy. Man is capable of only one orgasm and he loses energy, looks depressed. Even the next morning you can see his hangover, and as he goes on growing older it becomes more and more difficult. This difference has to be understood. The woman is on the receptive end—she has to be, because in nature's plan she is to become a mother, she needs more energy. But her orgasm has a totally different way of happening. Man's sexuality is local, like local anesthesia. A woman's body is sexual all over, and unless her whole body starts trembling with joy, each cell of her body starts becoming involved, she cannot have an orgasmic explosion.

So it is not only in your case that the man is boring, it is the case for almost ninety-nine percent of women around the world. The whole situation has to be changed. The woman should not be under the man. In the first place it is ugly—the man has a stronger body, the woman is more fragile. She should be on top of the man, not the man on top of her.

Secondly, the man should remain silent, inactive, so that his orgasm is not finished within two minutes. If you are silent and let the woman go crazy on top of your chest it will give her good exercise and it will bring her to an explosion of orgasmic energy. It takes time for her whole body to warm up, and if you are too active there is no time. You meet, but the meeting is not of beauty, of love, but just utilitarian.

Try with your girlfriend what I am saying. You be the inactive partner and let her be the active partner. Allow her to be uninhibited. She has not to behave like a lady, she has to behave like an authentic woman. The "lady" is just created by men; the woman is created by existence. And you have to fill the gap between her orgasms. The gap can be filled in only one way, that you remain very inactive, silent, and enjoy her going crazy. And she will have multiple orgasms. You should end the game with your orgasm, but you should not begin with it.

Then your girlfriend will not call you a little boring. You will be a really interesting, wonderful guy who is behaving like a lady! And keep your eyes closed so that she is not inhibited by your eyes. So she can do anything—moving her hands, her body, moaning, groaning, shouting. You are not allowed to be alive, you simply remain silent. Then she will be mad after you! Right now you must be behaving stupidly, as most of the men in the world do.

Your girlfriend is giving you good advice, and you in your stupidity are thinking that she is condemning you. When she says, "You are dependent and a victim," I can see even through your question that she is right. A victim you are, just as every human being is a victim—a victim of stupid ideologies, which have created strange guilt feelings and do not allow you to be playful. Although you may be making love, you know you are committing a sin and hell is not far off.

While making love, make it a meditative process. Your whole presence has to be there, showering on the woman you love. The woman has to be there, showering all her beauty and grace on her lover. Then you will not be a victim, otherwise you are, because love is not accepted by your idiotic religions to be a natural and playful experience. They condemn it. Some of them have made it a condition that unless you leave the woman you will never attain to truth. And the conditioning has been going on for so long that it has almost become a truth, although it is an absolute lie.

You are a victim of traditions and you are certainly dependent. When I read your question further you will see how you are dependent, dependent on a girlfriend who tells you that you are boring, not very juicy, and a victim.

Your dependence shows further: "Then I felt very guilty and depressed and utterly unworthy." If your girlfriend, by saying such simple truths, can make you feel guilty and depressed and utterly unworthy, she certainly seems to be your master. "I began to feel inside me a big no." And this is where your girlfriend has been kind, not to say to you, "You are a little bit of an idiot too."

You are saying, "I began to feel inside me a big no towards existence." Now what has existence done—towards life, towards love"? This shows your utter idiocy. Rather than listening to your girlfriend who was saying sincerely that you are boring, just a little, you should have asked her, "In what way can I become a little more interesting? Do you have any suggestions?" That would have been an intelligent step.

But instead of asking the girl you started having "a big no: towards existence, life, love." But I understand the reason. Perhaps you may not be able to explain it, but I can see the underlying reason for your big "no." You believe in your girlfriend too much. Naturally, you could not ask her; that would show your dependence. You must be afraid to make much fuss about these things with her, because girlfriends are not your permanent wives; no law prevents them from moving with someone who is more juicy. And everybody in the beginning is juicy, but just a few days together and the whole juice dries out. You start looking around for some other woman, for some other man, because they all look juicier.

You will repeat the same thing life after life; you have done it already, without understanding the foundation. Living with one man more than a week the problem arises of how to get rid of him. He is also thinking about how to get rid of you. But it does not look right to either of you, so you start creating trouble so that somehow some other idiot may become interested in your girlfriend, because you both go on seeing that other girls are more juicy, other men are more juicy. It is an old story that the grass on the other side of the fence looks greener than your own grass. Distance creates that phenomenon.

Any woman may look to you more interesting than your wife; she is just a pain in the neck. But what you don't know is that all these women are following the same philosophy. For one or two days they are so wonderful, and once they have caught hold of you the real story starts—they start becoming a pain in the neck. The same is true about men. Meeting a woman on the beach, in the park, by the side of a river, he pretends to be Alexander the Great, walks like a lion. And within two days the same fellow is reduced to a rat.

Nobody talks about the reality of why this is happening, why so many people are unnecessarily made miserable. This society will never be happy if we don't allow people to move and not get stuck in marriages, not get stuck in their own promises.

Out of freedom meet with each other, and the moment you feel that you have explored the whole topography of the woman and the woman knows that she has experienced whatever is possible to experience in the man, then it is time to say good-bye to each other in deep friendliness. There is no need to hang around each other's neck.

A world completely free from any contracts between man and woman will be immensely lovely, beautiful, unboring, interesting. But we have created institutions, and to live in an institution is not a very great experience. Your marriage is an institution, although the newer generation is moving a little more freely, before settling after the age of thirty. I have been looking around the world to find a hippie who is at least thirty-five years old. I have not found any. Around thirty, all hippies disappear; they become just the same conservative people whom they were fighting against before.

Seeing the situation that living in institutions is—marriage, community, society, Lions Club, Rotary Club—you cannot live joyously, you have experimented. This is the first time in history that we have a younger generation. I don't mean that in the past there were not young people, but there was no "younger generation." A small child, seven years old, would start following the father's business, would start going to the fields, taking care of the cows; or if the father was a carpenter, the child would start helping him. At the age of seven he had already joined the society.

For the first time in history there is a generation which can be authentically called younger, and which has created a generation gap. Schools are there, colleges are there, universities, and it takes twenty-five years, twenty-six years to come out of the university with a postgraduate degree. But by that time you are no longer young. By that time you start having responsibilities: profession, family, marriage.

But during the time that you spend in the universities, before entering life, there is a long gap in which you are not engaged in any utilitarian, purposive activity. That has created the generation gap. Men and women become sexually mature—women by the age of thirteen, men by the age of fourteen—and they will be married perhaps ten or twelve years afterwards. These twelve years have made girlfriends and boyfriends possible.

It is a great opportunity for the future to understand the whole phenomenon and its psychology. You have the choice to change the old habits, to create trouble but drop old habits. Every man needs to be aware of many women. Every woman needs the experience of many other men before deciding to marry. Their experience will help them to find the right person with whom they can melt and merge without any difficulty.

"Meanwhile," you are saying, "I observed in me this destructive energy and I felt that I somehow enjoyed it!" Everybody has destructive energy, because energy, if left to itself, is bound to be destructive unless it is used with awareness and becomes creative. But the most important thing that you are saying is that, "Somehow I enjoyed it."

Then how are you going to change it? With anything that you enjoy you are bound to remain on the same level; you cannot change it, because you may not enjoy the change. And all this has come to your mind only because your girlfriend told you that you are "a little boring, very dependent, and a victim."

You have energy. To enjoy destructive energy is suicidal, to enjoy destructive energy as destructive is in the service of death. If you are aware of it you have to go through a transformation. Use your energy creatively; perhaps that will make you less boring, more interesting, less dependent, less of a victim. And the most important part will be that you will not feel guilty and depressed. No creative person feels depressed and guilty. His participation in the universe through his creative actions makes him tremendously fulfilled and gives him dignity. That is the very birthright of every human being, but very few people claim it.

Moreover, this big "no" will become a big "yes" if the energy moves into creative dimensions. And there is no difficulty, it is so easy to use energy in creative fields. Paint, do gardening, grow flowers, write poetry, learn music, dance. Learn anything that changes your destructive energy into creative energy, and immediately the big no will become even a bigger yes. Then you will not be angry at existence, you will be grateful. You will not be against life.

How can a creative person be against life, love? It is impossible, it has never happened. It is only the uncreative people who are against everything. And if you can be creative, life-affirmative, you will have moved in the direction of becoming an authentic, sincere, celebrating individual.

Your girlfriend has raised very important questions for your life. The easiest way would be to change the girlfriend, but I suggest that she is certainly a friend to you and that whatever she has said is absolutely sincere, authentic. Be grateful to her and start changing things. The day your girlfriend accepts you as alive, interesting, will be a great day in your life. So don't be a coward and change girlfriends just because this one creates trouble in your mind, and you want to find some other one.

You are fortunate to find a very compassionate woman. Your next choice will be very difficult; she will make you feel absolutely guilty and unworthy, because what have you done to be worthy? What have you done not to be boring? What have you done to declare your independence? What have you done not to be a victim? It is time you should do it. You will remain always grateful to your girlfriend.

And I would like to tell your girlfriend, "Go on hitting this fellow until you are satisfied that he is not boring but full of life, utterly interesting, playful, celebrating. You may lose him somewhere on the path of life, but you will have prepared him for some other woman; otherwise the way he is now he is going to torture many women and torture himself."

I am trying to prepare the future man, who will respect the woman as equal to himself, who will give opportunity for her growth as he takes opportunity for his own growth. And there will not be any kind of bondage. If two persons can live in love their whole life, nobody is going to disturb them. But there is no need of any marriage and there is no need of any divorce. Love should be an absolute act of freedom.

But you have also been told for thousands of years that, "If you really love then your love has to be permanent." I don't see that anything in life has the quality of being permanent. Love cannot be an exception. So don't expect that love has to be permanent. It will make your love life more beautiful, because you know today you are together, tomorrow perhaps you will have to depart. Love comes like a fresh, fragrant breeze into your home, fills it with freshness and fragrance, remains as long as existence allows it and then moves out. You should not try to close all your doors or the same fresh breeze will become absolutely stale.

That's what people's lives have become—stale, ugly—and the reason lies in their idea of permanent love. In life everything is changing. And change is beautiful; it gives you more and more experience, more and more awareness, more and more maturity.

?

All the joy and fun has gone out of my relationship, although I feel the love is still there and I don't really want us to break up. How can we put that joy and fun back into our relationship?

There is some misunderstanding in your mind. The joy is not gone, joy has never been there—it was something else. It is excitement that has gone, but you thought that excitement was joy. The joy will come now; when the excitement subsides, only then does joy come. Joy is a very silent phenomenon; it is not excitement at all, it is not feverish at all. It is tranquil, calm and cool.

But this misunderstanding is not unique to you; it has become very prevalent. People think that excitement is joy. It is a kind of intoxication; one feels occupied, tremendously occupied. In that occupation one forgets one's worries, problems, anxieties. It is like drinking alcohol: you forget your problems, you forget yourself, and at least for the moment you are far, far away from yourself. That is the meaning of excitement: you are no longer inside, you are outside yourself; you have escaped from yourself. But because of this being outside yourself, sooner or later you become tired. You miss the nourishment that comes from your innermost core when you are close to it.

So no excitement can be permanent; it can only be a moment's phenomenon, a momentary thing. All honeymoons end; they have to end, otherwise you will be killed! If you remain excited you will go berserk. It has to subside, you have to be nourished within yourself again. One cannot remain awake for many nights in a row. For one night, two nights, three nights it is okay, but if you remain awake for too many nights you will start feeling tired, utterly tired and exhausted. And you will start feeling dull and dead too; you will need rest. After each excitement there is a need for rest. In rest you recapitulate, you recover; then you can move into excitement again.

But excitement is not joy, it is just an escape from misery.

Try to understand it very clearly: excitement is just an escape from misery. It gives only a false and superficial experience of joy. Because you are no longer miserable you think you are joyous; not to be miserable is equivalent to being joyous. Real joy is a positive phenomenon. Not to be miserable is just a kind of forgetfulness. The misery is waiting back home for you, and whenever you come back it will be there.

When excitement disappears, one starts thinking, "Now what is the point of this love?" What people call "love" dies with excitement, and that is a calamity. In fact, love had never been born. It was just a love of excitement; it was not real love. It was just an effort to move away from yourself. It was a search for sensation.

You rightly use the word "fun" in your question; it was fun, but it was not intimacy. When excitement disappears and you just start feeling loving, love can grow; now the feverish days are over. This is the true beginning of love.

To me, the true love begins when the honeymoon is over. But by that time your mind thinks that all is over, finished: "Search for another woman, search for another man. Now what is the point in continuing? There is no more fun!"

If you go on loving now, love will take on a depth, it will

become intimacy. A quality of grace will arise in it. It will have a subtlety now, it will not be superficial. It will not be fun, it will be meditation, it will be prayerfulness. It will help you to know yourself. The other will become a mirror, and through her you will be able to know yourself. Now is the time, the right time for love to grow because all the energy that was being channeled into excitement will not be wasted: it will be poured into the very roots of love, and the tree will be able to have great foliage.

If you can go on growing in this intimacy, which is no longer excitement, then joy will arise: first excitement, then love, then joy. Joy is the ultimate product, the fulfillment. Excitement is just a beginning, a trigger; it is not the end. And those who finish things at excitement will never know what love is, will never know the mystery of love, will never come to know the joy of love. They will know sensations, excitement, passionate fever, but they will never know the grace that is love. They will never know how beautiful it is to be with a person with no excitement but with silence, with no words, with no effort to do anything. Just being together, sharing one space, one being, sharing each other, not thinking of what to do and what to say, where to go and how to enjoy; all those things are gone. The storm is over and there is silence.

And it is not that you will not make love, but it will not be a "making" really; it will be love happening. It will happen out of grace, out of silence, out of a rhythm; it will arise from your depths, it will not be of the body, really. There is a sex that is spiritual, which has nothing to do with the body. Although the body partakes in it, participates in it, it is not the source of it. Then sex takes on the color of Tantra—and only then.

So my suggestion is: watch yourself. Now that you are coming closer to the temple don't escape. Go into it. Forget excitement, it is just childish. And something beautiful is ahead. If you can wait for it, if you have patience and can trust in it, it will come.

ATTRACTION AND OPPOSITION

There are a few very fundamental things to be understood.

First, a man and a woman are on the one hand halves of the other, and on the other hand, opposite polarities. Their being opposites attracts them to each other. The farther away they are, the deeper will be the attraction; the more different from each other they are, the more will be the charm and beauty and attraction.

But there lies the whole problem. When they come close, they want to come closer, they want to merge into each other, they want to become one, a harmonious whole, but their whole attraction depends on opposition, and the harmony will depend on dissolving the opposition. Unless a love affair is very conscious, it is going to create great anguish, great trouble.

All lovers are in trouble. The trouble is not personal; it is in the very nature of things.

They would not have been attracted to each other—they call it "falling in love." They cannot give any reason why they have such a tremendous pull toward each other. They are not even conscious of the underlying causes; hence a strange thing happens: the happiest lovers are those who never meet! Once they meet, the same opposition that created the attraction becomes a conflict. On each small point, their attitudes are different, their approaches are different. Although they speak the same language, they cannot understand each other.

One of my friends was talking to me about his wife and their continuous conflict. I said, "It seems you cannot understand each other."

He said, "What to say about *under*standing her, I cannot even *stand* her!" And it was a love marriage, not arranged. The parents of both were opposed to it; they belonged to two different religions, their societies were opposed to any intermarriage between them. But they fought against everybody and got married, only to find that they had entered into a constant struggle.

The way the male mind looks at the world is different from the female mind. For example, the male mind is interested in faraway things: in the future of humanity, in the faraway stars, whether there are living beings on other planets or not. A feminine mind simply giggles at the whole nonsense. She is only interested in a small, close circle around her—in the neighbors, in the family, in who is cheating on his wife, whose wife has fallen in love with the chauffeur. Her interest is local and human. She is not worried about reincarnation; neither is she concerned about life after death. The feminine concerns are more pragmatic, more concerned with the present, with the here and now.

A man is never here and now, he is always somewhere else. He has strange preoccupations: reincarnation, life after death, life on other planets.

If both partners are conscious of the fact that it is a meeting of opposites, that there is no need to make it a conflict, then it is a great opportunity to understand the totally opposite point of view and absorb it. Then the life of a man and woman together can become a beautiful harmony. Otherwise, it is continuous fight.

There are holidays. One cannot continue to fight twenty-four hours a day; one needs a little rest too, a rest to get ready for a new fight.

But it is one of the strangest phenomena that for thousands of years men and women have been living together, yet they are strangers. They go on giving birth to children, but still they remain strangers. The feminine approach and the masculine approach are so opposed to each other that unless a conscious effort is made, unless it becomes your meditation, there is no hope of having a peaceful life.

It is one of my deep concerns: how to make love and meditation so involved in each other that each love affair automatically becomes a partnership in meditation, and each meditation makes you so conscious that you need not fall in love, you can rise in love. You can find a friend consciously, deliberately. Your love will deepen as your meditation deepens, and vice versa: as your meditation blossoms, your love will also blossom. But it is on a totally different level.

But most couples are not connected in meditation. They never sit silently for one hour together just to feel each other's consciousness. Either they are fighting or they are making love, but in both cases, they are related with the body, the physical part, the biology, the hormones. They are not related with the innermost core of the other. Their souls remain separate.

In the temples and in the churches and in the courts, only your bodies are married. Your souls are miles apart. While you are making love to your partner, even in those moments neither are you there, nor is your partner there. Perhaps the man is thinking of Cleopatra, some movie actress. And perhaps that's why every woman keeps her eyes closed: not to see her husband's face, not to get disturbed. She is thinking of Alexander the Great, Ivan the Terrible, and looking at her husband, everything falls apart. He looks just like a mouse.

Even in those beautiful moments which should be sacred, meditative, of deep silence—even then you are not alone with your beloved. There is a crowd. Your mind is thinking of somebody else, your partner's mind is thinking of somebody else. Then what you are doing is just robotlike, mechanical. Some biological force is enslaving you, and you call it love.

I have heard that early in the morning, a drunkard on the beach saw a man doing pushups. The drunkard walked around him, looked very closely from here and from there, and finally said, "I should not interfere in such an intimate affair, but I have to tell you that your girlfriend has gone!"

That seems to be the situation. When you are making love, is your woman really there? Is your man really there? Or are you just doing a ritual, something which has to be done, a duty to be fulfilled?

If you want a harmonious relationship with your partner, you will have to learn to be more meditative. Love alone is not enough. Love alone is blind; meditation gives it eyes. Meditation gives it understanding. And once your love is both love and meditation, you become fellow travelers. Then it is no longer an ordinary relationship. Then it becomes a friendliness on the path towards discovering the mysteries of life.

Man alone, woman alone, will find the journey very tedious and very long, as they have found it in the past. Because seeing this continuous conflict, all the religions decided that those who wanted to seek should renounce the other—the monks should be celibate, the nuns should be celibate. But in five thousand years of history, how many monks and how many nuns have become realized souls? You cannot even give me names enough to count on ten fingers. And there have been millions of monks and nuns of all religions: Buddhist, Hindu, Christian, Mohammedan. What has happened?

The path is not so long, the goal is not that far away. But even if you want to go to your neighbor's house you will need both your legs. Just jumping on one leg, how far can you go?

Men and women together in deep friendship, in a loving, meditative relationship, as organic wholes, can reach the goal any moment they want. Because the goal is not outside you; it is the center of the cyclone, it is the innermost part of your being. But you can find it only when you are whole, and you cannot be whole without the other.

Man and woman are two parts of one whole. So rather than wasting time in fighting, try to understand each other. Try to put yourself in the place of the other; try to see as a man sees, try to see as a woman sees. And four eyes are always better than two eyes. You have a full view; all four directions are available to you.

But one thing has to be remembered: that without meditation, love is destined to fail; there is no possibility of its being a success. You can pretend and you can deceive others, but you cannot deceive yourself. You know deep down that all the promises love had given to you have remained unfulfilled.

Only with meditation does love start taking on new colors, new music, new songs, new dances, because meditation gives you the insight to understand the polar opposite, and in that very understanding the conflict disappears.

All the conflict in the world is because of misunderstanding. You say something, your wife understands something else. Your wife says something, you understand something else. I have seen couples who have lived together for thirty or forty years; still, they seem to be as immature as they were on their first day together. Still the same complaint: "She doesn't understand what I am saying." Forty years being together and you have not been able to figure out some way that your wife can understand exactly what you are saying, and you can understand exactly what she is saying?

But I think there is no possibility for it to happen except through meditation, because meditation gives you the qualities of silence, awareness, a patient listening, a capacity to put yourself in the other's position.

Things are not impossible, but we have not tried the right medicine.

I would like you to be reminded that the word "medicine" comes from the same root as "meditation." Medicine cures your body; meditation cures your soul. Medicine heals the material part of you; meditation heals the spiritual part of you.

People are living together and their spirits are full of wounds; hence, small things hurt them so much.

Mulla Nasruddin was asking me, "What to do? Whatever I say I am misunderstood, and immediately there is trouble."

I said, "Try one thing: just sit silently, don't say anything."

The next day, I saw him in more despair than ever. I said, "What happened?"

He said, "I should not ask you for advice. Every day we used to fight and quarrel, but it was just verbal. Yesterday, because of your advice, I got beaten!"

I said, "What happened?"

He said, "I just sat there silent. She asked many questions, but I was determined to remain silent. She said, 'So you are not going to speak?' I remained silent. So she started hitting me with things! And she was very angry. She said, 'Things have gone from bad to worse. At least we used to talk to each other; now even we are not on speaking terms!' The whole neighborhood gathered, and they all started asking, 'What happened? Why aren't you speaking?' And somebody suggested: 'It seems he is possessed by some evil spirit.'

"I thought, my God, now they are going to take me to some idiot who will beat me and try to drive the evil spirit out. I said, 'Wait! I'm not possessed by any evil spirit, I'm simply not speaking because to say anything triggers a fight: I say something, then she has to say something, and then I have to say something, and nobody knows where it is going to end.' I was simply meditating silently, doing no harm to anybody, and suddenly the whole neighborhood was against me!"

People are living without any understanding. Hence, whatsoever they do is going to end in disaster.

If you love a man, meditation will be the best present that you can give to him. If you love a woman, then the Kohinoor is nothing; meditation will be a far more precious gift, and it will make your life sheer joy.

We are potentially capable of sheer joy, but we don't know how to manage it.

Alone, we are at the most sad. Together, it becomes really hell.

Even a man like Jean-Paul Sartre, a man of great intelligence, has to say that the other is hell, that to be alone is better, you cannot make it with the other. He became so pessimistic that he said it is impossible to make it with the other, the other is hell. Ordinarily, he is right.

With meditation the other becomes your heaven. But Jean-Paul Sartre had no idea of meditation.

That is the misery of Western man. Western man is missing the flowering of life because he knows nothing about meditation, and Eastern man is missing because he knows nothing of love. And to me, just as man and woman are halves of one whole, so are love and meditation. Meditation is man; love is woman. In the meeting of meditation and love is the meeting of man and woman. And in that meeting, we create the transcendental human being, which is neither man nor woman. And unless we create the transcendental man on the earth, there is not much hope.

?

You have spoken about the ultimate harmony to be found in what seem to be opposites, but I feel that hate destroys love and anger kills compassion. When these extremes are fighting inside me, how can I find the harmony?

You are caught in a misunderstanding. If hate destroys love and anger destroys compassion then there is no possibility for love or compassion to exist. Then you are caught, then you cannot get out of it. You have lived with hate for millions of lives, so it must have destroyed love already. You have lived with anger for millions of lives, so it must have murdered compassion already.

But look, love is still there. Hate comes and goes, and love survives. Anger comes and goes, and compassion survives. Hate has not been able to destroy love; night has not been able to destroy the day, and darkness has not been able to murder the light. No, they survive.

So the first thing to understand is that love and compassion have not been destroyed. The second thing, to understand the harmony of opposites, will be possible only later on, when you really love.

You have not really loved, that is the trouble. Not hate; hate is not the trouble, the trouble is that you have not really loved. Darkness is not the trouble, the trouble is that you don't have light. If light is there, darkness disappears. You have not loved. You fantasize, you imagine, you dream, but you have not loved.

Love! And I'm not saying that just by loving, the hate will immediately disappear—no. Hate will fight against you, because everybody wants to survive. Hate will struggle. The more you love, the stronger hate will come back with its struggle. But you will be surprised to discover that the hate comes and goes. It doesn't kill your love; rather, it makes love stronger. Love can absorb hate also. If you love a person, in some moments you can hate the same person. But that doesn't destroy love, it brings a richness to love.

What is hate in fact? It is a tendency to go away. What is love? A tendency to come closer. Hate is a tendency to separate, a tendency to divorce. Love is a tendency to marry, to come near, to become closer, to become one. Hate is to become two, independent. Love is to become one, interdependent. Whenever you hate, you go away from your lover, from your beloved. But in ordinary life going away is needed to come back again.

It is just like when you eat: You are hungry, so you eat; then hunger goes because you have eaten. When you love a person it is like food. Love is food—very subtle, spiritual, but it is food and it nourishes you. When you love a person the hunger subsides; you feel satiated, then suddenly the impulse to go away arises and you separate. But then you will feel hungry again; you would like to come nearer, closer, to love, to fall into each other. You eat, then for a few hours you forget about food; you don't go on sitting in the kitchen, you don't go on sitting in the restaurant. You go away; then after a few hours suddenly you start coming back. Hunger is arising.

Love has two faces, one of hunger and one of satiety. You misunderstand love as only hunger. Once you understand that there is no hate, but only a situation to create hunger, then hate becomes part of love. Then it enriches love. Then anger becomes part of compassion, it enriches compassion. A compassion without any possibility of anger will be impotent, it will have no energy in it. A compassion with the possibility of anger has strength, stamina. A love without the possibility of hate will become stale. Then the partnership will look like an imprisonment, you cannot get away. A love with hate has a freedom in it; it never becomes stale.

In the mathematics of life, divorces happen because every day you go on postponing them. Then divorce goes on accumulating and one day the marriage is completely killed by it, destroyed by it. If you understand me, I would suggest to you not to wait: every day divorce and remarry. It should be a rhythm just like day and night, hunger and satiety, summer and winter, life and death. It should be like that. In the morning you love, in the afternoon you hate. When you love you really love, you totally love; when you hate you really hate, you totally hate. And suddenly you will find the beauty of it: the beauty is in the totality.

A total hate is also beautiful, as beautiful as total love; a total anger is also beautiful, as beautiful as total compassion. The beauty is in totality. Anger alone becomes ugly, hate alone becomes ugly—it is just the valley without the hill, without the peak. But with the peak the valley becomes a beautiful scene. From the peak the valley becomes lovely, from the valley the peak becomes lovely.

You move; your life river moves between these two banks. And, by and by, the more and more you understand the mathematics of life, you won't think that hate is against love. It is complementary. You won't think that anger is against compassion; it is complementary. Then you don't think that rest is against work, it is complementary; or that night is against day; it is complementary. They make a perfect whole.

Because you have not loved, you are afraid of hate. You are afraid because your love is not strong enough. Hate could destroy it. You are not certain, really, whether you love or not; that's why you are afraid of hate and anger. You know that it may completely shatter the whole house. You are not certain whether the house really exists or is just imagination, an imaginary house. If it is imagination the hate will destroy it; if it is real the hate will make it stronger. After the storm a silence descends. After hate, lovers are again fresh to fall into each other completely fresh, as if they are meeting for the first time again. Again and again they meet, again and again for the first time.

Lovers are always meeting for the first time. If you meet a second time, then love is already getting old, stale. It is getting boring. Lovers always fall in love every day, fresh, young. You look at your woman and you cannot even recognize that you have seen her before—so new! You look at your man and he seems to be a stranger; you fall in love again.

Hate does not destroy love, it only destroys the staleness of it. It is a cleaning, and if you understand it you will be grateful to it. And if you can be grateful to hate also, you have understood; now nothing can destroy your love. Now you are for the first time really rooted; now you can absorb the storm and can be strengthened through it, can be enriched through it.

Don't look at life as a duality, don't look at life as a conflict—it is not. I have known—it is not. I have experienced—it is not. It is one whole, one piece, and everything fits in it. You have just to find out how to let them fit, how to allow them to fit. Allow them to fit into each other. It is a beautiful whole.

And if you ask me, if there were a possibility of a world without hate I would not choose it; it would be absolutely dead and boring. It might be sweet, but too sweet; you would hanker for salt. If a world were possible without anger I would not choose it, because just compassion without anger would have no life in it. The opposite gives the tension, the opposite gives the temper. When ordinary iron passes through fire it becomes steel; without fire it cannot become steel. And the higher the degree of temperature, the greater will be the temper, the strength, of the steel. If your compassion can pass through anger, the higher the temperature of the anger the greater will be the temper and the strength of the compassion.

Buddha is compassionate. He is a warrior. He comes from the *kshatriya* race, a samurai. He must have led a very angry life—and then suddenly, compassion. The Jain master Mahavir comes from a *kshatriya* clan. On the face of it this looks absurd, but it has a certain consistency to it: all the great teachers of nonviolence have come from the warrior races. They talk about nonviolence, compassion; they have lived violence, they know what violence is, they have passed through it. Only a *kshatriya*, a warrior, who has lived through fire, has such a strong compassion or the possibility for it.

So remember, if inside your heart these extremes are fighting, don't choose. Allow them both to be there. Be a big house, have enough room inside. Don't say, "I will have only compassion, not anger; I will have only love, not hate." You will be impoverished.

Have a big heart, let them both be there. There is no need to create a fight between them; there *is* no fight. The fight comes from your mind, from your teachings, upbringing, conditioning. The whole world goes on saying to you, "Love, don't hate." How can you love without hate? Jesus says, "Love your enemies." And I tell you, "Hate your lovers also." Then it becomes a complete whole. Otherwise Jesus' saying is incomplete. He says, "Love your enemies." You only hate your enemies, and he says you should love them also. But the other part is missing. I tell you, hate your friends also; hate your lovers also, and don't be afraid. Then by and by you will see there is no difference between the enemy and the friend, because you hate and love the enemy and you love and hate the friend. It will be only a question of the coin upside down or downside up. Then the friend is the enemy and the enemy is the friend. Then distinctions simply disappear.

Don't create a fight inside, allow them both to be there. They both will be needed. Both will give you two wings; only then can you fly.

DROPPING OUT OF THE LONELY HEARTS CLUB

A very intricate, complex thing has to be understood: If you are not in love, you are lonely. If you are in love, really in love, you become alone.

Loneliness is sadness; aloneness is not sadness. Loneliness is a feeling of incompleteness. You need someone and the needed one is not available. Loneliness is darkness, with no light in it. A dark house, waiting and waiting for someone to come and kindle the light.

Aloneness is not loneliness. Aloneness means the feeling that you are complete. Nobody is needed, you are enough. And this happens in love. Lovers become alone. Through love you touch your inner completeness. Love makes you complete. Lovers share each other, but that is not their need, that is their overflowing energy.

Two persons who have been feeling lonely can make a contract, can come together. They are not lovers, remember. They remain lonely but now, because of the presence of the other, they don't feel the loneliness, that's all. They somehow deceive themselves. Their love is nothing but a deception to deceive themselves: "I am not lonely, somebody else is there."

Because two lonely persons are meeting, their loneliness basically is doubled, or even multiplied. That's what happens ordinarily. You feel lonely when you are alone, and when you are in relationship you feel miserable. This is an everyday observation. When people are not in a relationship they feel lonely, and they are searching for somebody to be related to. When they are related to somebody, then the misery starts; then they feel it was better to be alone—this is too much.

What happens? Two lonely people meet—that means two gloomy, sad, miserable people meet—and the misery is multiplied. How can two uglinesses become beautiful? How can two lonelinesses coming together bring a sense of completion, totality? Not possible. They exploit each other, they somehow try to deceive themselves through being related to each other, but that deception doesn't go far. By the time the honeymoon is finished, the marriage is also finished. It is just a temporary illusion.

Real love is not a search to combat loneliness. Real love is to transform loneliness into aloneness, to help the other. If you love a person, you help that person to be alone. You don't try to fill him or her. You don't try to complete the other in some way by your presence. You help the other to be alone, to be so full out of her or his own being that you will not be needed.

When a person is totally free, then out of that freedom sharing is possible. Then he gives much, but not as a need; he gives much, but not as a bargain. He gives much because he has much. He gives because he enjoys giving.

Lovers are alone, and a real lover never destroys your aloneness. He will always be totally respectful toward your individuality, toward your aloneness. It is sacred. He will not interfere in it, he will not try to intrude on that space.

But ordinarily, lovers, so-called lovers, are very much afraid of the other's aloneness, independence. They are very much afraid, because they think if the other is independent then they will not be needed, then they will be discarded. So the woman goes on trying to manage things so that her husband or boyfriend remains dependent. He should be always in need of her, so that she can remain valuable. And the man goes on trying in every way to manage the same, so that he remains valuable. The result is a bargain, not love, and there is continuous conflict, struggle. The struggle is based in the fact that everybody needs freedom.

Love allows freedom; not only allows, but strengthens freedom. And anything that destroys freedom is not love. It must be something else. Love and freedom go together, they are two wings of the same bird. Whenever you see that your love is going against your freedom, then you are doing something else in the name of love.

Let this be your criterion: freedom is the criterion; love gives you freedom, makes you free, liberates you. And once you are totally yourself, you feel grateful to the person who has helped you. That gratefulness is almost religious. You feel in the other person something divine. He has made you free, she has made you free, and love has not become possessiveness.

When love deteriorates it becomes possessiveness, jealousy, struggle for power, politics, domination, manipulation—a thousand and one things, all ugly. When love soars high, to the purest sky, it is freedom, total freedom.

If you are in love, the love I am talking about, your very love will help the other to be integrated. Your very love will become a cementing force for the other. In your love the other will come together as a whole, unique and individual, because your love will give freedom. Under the shade of your love, under the protection of your love, the other will start growing.

All growth needs love, but *unconditional* love. If love has conditions then growth cannot be total, because those conditions will come in the way.

Love unconditionally, don't ask anything in return. Much comes back to you on its own—that's another thing—but don't be a beggar. In love, be an emperor. Just give it and see what happens: a thousandfold it comes back. But one has to learn the knack. Otherwise one remains a miser; one gives a little and waits for something to come back, and that waiting and expectation destroys the whole beauty of it.

When you are waiting and expecting, the other feels that you are being manipulative. He may say it or not, but he feels you are manipulating. And wherever you feel the other is trying to manipulate you, you want to rebel against it because it goes against the inner need of the soul, because any demand from the outside dis-integrates you. Any demand from the outside divides you. Any demand from the outside is a crime against you, because your freedom is polluted. Then you are no longer sacred. You are no longer the end, you are being used as a means. And the most immoral act in the world is to use somebody as a means.

Each being is an end unto himself. Love treats you as an end unto yourself. You are not to be dragged into any expectations.

So there are a few things to be remembered. One is to love, but not as a need—as a sharing. Love, but don't expect; give. Love, but remember your love should not become an imprisonment for the other. Love, but be very careful; you are moving on sacred ground. You are going into the highest, the purest and holiest temple. Be alert! Drop all impurities outside the temple. When you love a person, love the person as if the person is a god, not less than that. Never love a woman as a woman and never love a man as a man, because if you love a man as a man your love is going to be very ordinary. Your love is not going to be more than lust. If you love a woman as a woman, your love is not going to soar very high. Love a woman as a goddess, then love becomes worship.

In Tantra, the man who is going to make love to the woman has to worship her for months as a goddess. He has to visualize in the woman the mother-goddess. When the visualization has become total, when no lust arises, when seeing the woman sitting naked before him he simply feels thrilled with a divine energy and no lust arises, the very form of the woman becomes divine, and all thoughts stop and only reverence is felt—only then he is allowed to make love.

It looks a little absurd and paradoxical. When there is no need to make love, then he is allowed to make love. When the woman has become a goddess, then he is allowed to make love because now love can soar high, love can become a climax, a crescendo. Now it will not be of the earth, it will not be of this world; it will not be of two bodies, it will be of two beings. It will be a meeting of two existences. Two souls will meet, merge, and mingle, and both will come out of it tremendously alone.

Aloneness means purity. Aloneness means that you are just yourself and nobody else. Aloneness means that you are pure gold; just gold and nothing else, just you. Love makes you alone. Loneliness will disappear, but aloneness will arise.

Loneliness is a state when you are ill with yourself, bored with yourself, tired of yourself, and you want to go somewhere and to forget yourself in being involved with somebody else. Aloneness is when you are thrilled just by your being. You are blissful just by being yourself. You need not go anywhere. Need has disappeared, you are enough unto yourself. But now, a new thing arises in your being. You have so much that you cannot contain it. You have to share, you have to give. And whoever accepts your gift, you will feel grateful that the person has accepted.

Lovers feel grateful that their love has been accepted. They feel thankful, because they were so full of energy and they needed someone to pour that energy into. When a flower blooms and releases its fragrance to the winds it feels grateful to the winds. The fragrance was growing more and more heavy on the flower, it was becoming almost a burden. It is just as if a woman is pregnant and nine months have passed and the child is not being born, is delaying. Now she is so burdened; she wants to share the child with the world.

That is the meaning of birth. Up to now the woman has been carrying the child within herself, it was nobody else's but her own. But now it is too much; she cannot contain it. It has to be shared; the child has to be shared with the world. The mother has to drop her miserliness. Once the child is out of the womb, it is no longer only the mother's; by and by the child will go away, and far away. It will become part of the great world.

The same happens when a cloud comes full of rainwater ready to shower, and when it showers, rains, the cloud feels unburdened and happy and grateful to the thirsty earth because it accepted the rain.

There are two types of love. One is the love that happens when you are feeling lonely: as a need, you go to the other. The other love arises when you are not feeling lonely, but alone. In the first case you go to get something; in the second case you go to give something. A giver is an emperor.

Love that arises out of aloneness is not ordinary love. It has nothing to do with lust, on the contrary it is the greatest transformation of lust into love. And love makes you individual. If it doesn't make you individual, if it tries to make you a slave, then it is not love; it is hate pretending love. Love of this type kills, destroys the individuality of the other. It makes you less of an individual, it pulls you down. You are not enhanced, you don't become graceful. You are being pulled into the mud, and everybody who is tangled up in that kind of relationship starts feeling that he is settling with something dirty.

Love should give you freedom; never settle for less. Love should make you completely free, a wanderer in the sky of freedom, with no roots attached anywhere. Love is not an attachment; lust is.

Meditation and love are the two ways to attain to the individuality I am talking about. Both are very deeply related. In fact they are both aspects of the same coin: love and meditation. If you meditate, sooner or later you will come upon love. If you meditate deeply, sooner or later you will start feeling a tremendous love arising in you that you have never known before: a new quality to your being, a new door opening. You have become a new flame and you want to share now.

If you love deeply, by and by you will become aware that your love is becoming more and more meditative. A subtle quality of silence is entering in you. Thoughts are disappearing, gaps appearing, silences. You are touching your own depth.

Love makes you meditative if it is on the right lines. Meditation makes you loving if it is on the right lines.

The darkness of loneliness cannot be fought directly. It is something essential for everyone to understand, that there are a few fundamental things which cannot be changed. This is one of the fundamentals: you cannot fight with darkness directly, with loneliness directly, with the fear of isolation directly. The reason is that all these things do not exist; they are simply absences of something, just as darkness is the absence of light.

You can go on fighting with this darkness your whole life and you will not succeed, but just a small candle is enough to dispel it. You have to work for the light because it is positive, existential; it exists on its own. And once light comes, anything that was its absence automatically disappears.

Loneliness is similar to darkness.

You don't know your aloneness. You have not experienced your aloneness and its beauty, its tremendous power, its strength. Loneliness and aloneness in the dictionaries are synonymous, but existence does not follow your dictionaries. And nobody has yet tried to make an existential dictionary which will not be contradictory to existence.

Loneliness is an absence, because you don't know your aloneness. There is fear. You feel lonely so you want to cling to something, to somebody, to some relationship, just to hold on to the illusion that you are not lonely. But you know you are, hence the pain. On the one hand you are clinging to something that is not for real, which is just a temporary arrangement—a relationship, a friendship. And while you are in the relationship you can create a little illusion to forget your loneliness.

But this is the problem: although you can forget for a moment your loneliness, just the next moment you suddenly become aware that the relationship or the friendship is nothing permanent. Yesterday you did not know this man or this woman, you were strangers. Today you are friends; who knows about tomorrow? Tomorrow you may be strangers again, hence the pain.

The illusion gives a certain solace, but it cannot create the reality so that all fear disappears. It represses the fear, so on the surface you feel good—at least you try to feel good. You pretend to feel good to yourself: how wonderful is the relationship, how wonderful is the man or the woman. But behind the illusion—and the illusion is so thin that you can see behind it—there is pain in the heart, because the heart knows perfectly well that tomorrow things may not be the same, and they are not the same.

Your whole life's experience supports that things go on changing. Nothing remains stable; you cannot cling to anything in a changing world. You wanted to make your friendship something permanent but your wanting is against the law of change, and that law is not going to make exceptions. It simply goes on doing its own thing. It will change, everything will change. Perhaps in the long run you will understand one day that it was good that it did not listen to you, that existence did not bother about you and just went on doing whatever it wanted to do, not according to your desire.

It may take a little time for you to understand. You want this friend to be your friend forever, but tomorrow he turns into an enemy. Or simply, "You get lost!" and he is no longer with you. Somebody else fills the gap who is a far superior being. Then suddenly you realize it was good that the other one got lost; otherwise you would have been stuck with him. But still the lesson never goes so deep that you stop asking for permanence.

You will start asking for permanence with this man, with this woman: now this should not change. You have not really learned the lesson that change is simply the very fabric of life. You have to understand it and go with it. Don't create illusions; they are not going to help. And everybody is creating illusions of different kinds.

I used to know one man who said, "I trust only money, nothing else."

I said, "You are making a very significant statement."

He said, "Everybody changes. You cannot rely on anybody. And as you get older, only your money is yours. Nobody cares, not even your son, not even your wife. If you have money they all care, they all respect you because you have money. If you don't have money you become a beggar."

His saying that the only thing in the world to trust is money comes out of a long experience of life, of getting cheated again and again by the people he trusted. And he thought they loved him but they were all around him for the money.

"But," I told him, "at the moment of death money is not going to be with you. You can have an illusion that at least money is with you, but as your breathing stops, money is no longer with you. You have earned something but it will be left on this side; you cannot carry it beyond death. You will fall into a deep loneliness which you have been hiding behind the facade of money."

There are people who are after power, but the reason is the same: when they are in power so many people are with them, millions of people are under their domination. They are not alone. They are great political and religious leaders. But power changes. One day you have it, another day it is gone, and suddenly the whole illusion disappears. You are lonely as nobody else is, because others are at least accustomed to being lonely. You are not accustomed, your loneliness hurts you more.

Society has tried to make arrangements so you can forget loneliness. Arranged marriages are just an effort so that you know your wife is with you. All religions resist divorce for the simple reason that if divorce is allowed then the basic purpose marriage was invented for is destroyed. The basic purpose was to give you a companion, a lifelong companion.

But even though a wife will be with you or a husband will be with you for your whole life, that does not mean that love remains the same. In fact, rather than giving you a companion, they give you a burden to carry. You were lonely, already in trouble, and now you have to carry another person who is lonely. And in this life there is no hope, because once love disappears you both are lonely, and both have to tolerate each other. Now it is not a question of being enchanted by each other; at the most you can patiently tolerate each other. Your loneliness has not been changed by the social strategy of marriage.

Religions have tried to make you a member of an organized body of religion so you are always in a crowd. You know that there are millions of Catholics; you are not alone, millions of Catholics are with you. Jesus Christ is your savior. God is with you. Alone you may have been wrong, doubt may have arisen, but millions of people cannot be wrong. A little support, but even that is gone because there are millions who are not Catholics. There are the people who crucified Jesus, there are people who don't believe in God. And their number is not less than Catholics, it is more. There are other religions with different concepts. It is difficult for an intelligent person not to doubt. You may have millions of people following a certain belief system, but still you cannot be certain that they are with you, that you are not lonely.

God was a device, but all devices have failed. It was a device. . . . when nothing else is there, at least God is with you. He is always everywhere with you. In the dark night of the soul, he is with you, so don't be worried. It was good for a childish humanity to be deceived by this concept, but you cannot be deceived. This God who is always everywhere—you don't see him, you can't talk to him, you can't touch him. You don't have any evidence for his existence except your desire that he should be there. But your desire is not a proof of anything.

God is only a desire of the childish mind. Man has come of age, and God has become meaningless. The hypothesis has lost its grip.

What I am trying to say is that every effort that has been directed toward avoiding loneliness has failed, and will fail, because it is against the fundamentals of life. What is needed is not something in which you can forget your loneliness. What is needed is that you become aware of your aloneness, which is a reality. And it is so beautiful to experience it, to feel it, because it is your freedom from the crowd, from the other. It is your freedom from the fear of being lonely.

Just the word "lonely" immediately reminds you that it is like a wound: something is needed to fill it. There is a gap and it hurts, something needs to be put into that gap. The very word "aloneness" does not have the same sense of a wound, of a gap that has to be filled. Aloneness simply means completeness. You are whole; there is no need of anybody else to complete you.

So try to find your innermost center, where you are always alone, have always been alone. In life, in death, wherever you are you will be alone. But it is so full; it is not empty, it is so full and so complete and so overflowing with all the juices of life, with all the beauties and benedictions of existence that once you have tasted aloneness the pain in the heart will disappear. Instead, a new rhythm of tremendous sweetness, peace, joy, bliss, will be there.

It does not mean that a person who is centered in his aloneness, complete in himself, cannot make friends. In fact, only that person can make friends, because now it is no longer a need, it is just sharing. You have so much you can share.

And when you share, there is no question of clinging. You flow with existence, you flow with life's change, because it doesn't matter with whom you share. It can be the same person tomorrow—the same person for your whole life—or it can be different persons. It is not a contract, it is not a marriage; it is simply out of your fullness that you want to give. So whoever happens to be near you, you give. And giving is such a joy.

Begging is such a misery. Even if you get something through begging, you will remain miserable. It hurts. It hurts your pride, it hurts your integrity. But sharing makes you more centered, more integrated, more proud—but not more egoistic, simply proud that existence has been compassionate to you. It is not ego; it is a totally different phenomenon, a recognition that existence has allowed you something for which millions of people are trying but at the wrong door. You happen to be at the right door.

You are proud of your blissfulness and all that existence has given to you. Fear disappears, darkness disappears, the pain disappears, the desire for the other disappears. You can love a person, and if the person loves somebody else there will not be any jealousy, because you loved out of so much joy. It was not a clinging, you were not holding the other person in prison. You were not worried that the other person may slip out of your hands, that somebody else may start having a love affair. When you are sharing your joy, you don't create a prison for anybody. You simply give. You don't even expect gratitude or thankfulness because you are not giving to get anything, not even gratitude. You are giving because you are so full you have to give.

So I will not tell you to do anything about your loneliness. Look for your aloneness. Forget loneliness, forget darkness, forget pain. These are just the absence of aloneness, and the experience of aloneness will dispel them instantly. And the method is the same: just watch your mind, be aware. Become more and more conscious, so finally you are only conscious of yourself. That is the point where you become aware of aloneness.

And always look to see if anything that you are facing as a problem is a negative thing or a positive thing. If it is a negative thing then don't fight with it; don't bother about it at all. Just look for the positive of it, and you will be at the right door. Most of the people in the world miss because they start fighting directly with the negative door. There is no door; there is only darkness, there is only absence. And the more they fight the more they find failure, the more they become dejected, pessimistic, and ultimately they decide that life has no meaning, that it is simply torture. Their mistake is that they entered from the wrong door.

So before you face a problem, just look at it—is it an absence of something? And the truth is that all your problems are the absence of something. Once you have found what they are the absence of, then go after the positive. The moment you find the positive you have found the light, and the darkness is finished.

Why is it I feel fully alive only when I am in love? I tell myself that I should be able to spark myself without the other, but so far no luck. Is this some stupid *Waiting for Godot* game I am playing with myself? When the last love affair ended I swore to myself I was not going to let the same old deadening process happen, but here I am again feeling half alive, waiting for "him" to come.

One remains in need of the other up to that point, up to that experience, when one enters into one's own innermost core. Unless one knows oneself one remains in the need of the other. But the need of the other is very paradoxical; its nature is paradoxical. When you are alone you feel lonely, you feel the other is missed; your life seems to be only half. It loses joy, it loses flow, flowering; it remains undernourished. If you are with the other, then a new problem arises because the other starts encroaching on your space. He starts imposing conditions upon you, he starts demanding things from you, he starts destroying your freedom, and that hurts.

So when you are with somebody, only for a few days when the honeymoon is still there, and the more intelligent you are, the shorter will be the honeymoon, remember. Only for utterly dull people it can be a long affair; for insensitive people it can be a lifelong thing. But if you are intelligent, sensitive, soon you will realize what you have done. The other is destroying your freedom, and suddenly you become aware that you need your freedom because freedom is of immense value. And you decide never again to bother with the other.

Again when you are alone you are free, but something is missing, because your aloneness is not true aloneness; it is only loneliness, it is a negative state. You forget all about freedom. Free you are, but what to do with this freedom? Love is not there, and both are essential needs.

And up to now humanity has lived in such an insane way that you can fulfill only one need: either you can be free, but then you have to drop the idea of love. That's what monks and nuns of all the religions have been doing: drop the idea of love, you are free; there is nobody to hinder you, there is nobody to interfere with you, nobody to make any demands, nobody to possess you. But then their life becomes cold, almost dead.

You can go to any monastery and look at the monks and the nuns: their life is ugly. It stinks of death; it is not fragrant with life. There is no dance, no joy, no song. All songs have disappeared, all joy is dead. They are paralyzed—how can they dance? They are crippled—how can they dance? There is nothing to dance about. Their energies are stuck, they are no longer flowing. For the flow the other is needed; without the other there is no flow.

So the majority of humanity has decided for love and dropped the idea of freedom. But then people are living like slaves. Man has reduced the woman into a thing, a commodity, and of course the woman has done the same in her own subtle way: she has made all the husbands henpecked.

I have heard:

> *In New York a few henpecked husbands joined hands together. They made a club to protest, to fight—Men's Liberation Movement, or something like that! And of course they chose one of the most henpecked husbands the president of the club.*
>
> *The first meeting happened, but the president never turned up. They were all worried. They rushed to his home and they asked him, "What is the matter? Have you forgotten?"*
>
> *He said, "No, but my wife won't allow me. She says, 'You*

> *go out, and I will never allow you back in!' And that much risk I cannot take."*

The man has reduced the woman to a slave and the woman has reduced the man to a slave. And of course both hate the slavery, both resist it. They are constantly fighting; any small excuse and the fight starts.

But the real fight is somewhere else deep down; the real fight is that they are asking for freedom. They cannot say it so clearly, they may have forgotten completely. For thousands of years this is the way people have lived. They have seen their fathers and mothers living in the same way, they have seen their grandparents living in the same way. This is the way people live; they have accepted it, and their freedom is destroyed.

It is as if we are trying to fly in the sky with one wing. A few people have the wing of love and a few people have the wing of freedom, but both are incapable of flying. Both the wings are needed.

You are asking, "Why is it I feel fully alive only when I am in love?" It is perfectly natural; there is nothing wrong in it. It is how it should be. Love is a natural need; it is like food. If you are hungry, of course you will feel a deep unease. Without love your soul is hungry; love is a soul nourishment. Just as the body needs food, water, air, the soul needs love. But the soul also needs freedom, and it is one of the strangest things that we have not accepted this fact yet.

If you love there is no need to destroy your freedom. They both can exist together; there is no antagonism between them. It is because of our foolishness that we have created the antagonism. Hence, the monks think the worldly people are fools, and the worldly people deep down know that the monks are fools; they are missing all the joys of life.

A great priest was asked, "What is love?"

The priest said, "A word made up of two vowels, two consonants, and two fools!"

That is their condemnation of love. Because all the religions have condemned love, they have praised freedom very much. In India we call the ultimate experience *moksha; moksha* means absolute freedom.

You say: "I tell myself that I should be able to spark myself without the other, but so far no luck." It will remain so, it will not change. You should rather change your conditioning about love and freedom. Love the person, but give the person total freedom. Love the person, but from the very beginning make it clear that you are not selling your freedom.

And if you cannot make it happen in this community, here with me, you cannot make it happen anywhere else. Here we are experimenting with many things, and one of the dimensions of our experiment is to make love and freedom possible together, to support their coexistence together. Love a person but don't possess, and don't be possessed. Insist for freedom, and don't lose love! There is no need. There is no natural enmity between freedom and love; it is a created enmity. Of course for centuries it has been so, so you have become accustomed to it; it has become a conditioned thing.

An old farmer down South could barely speak above a whisper. Leaning on a fence by the side of a country road he was watching a dozen razorbacks in a patch of woodland. Every few minutes the hogs would scramble through a hole in the fence, tear across the road to another patch of woodland, and immediately afterward scurry back again.

"What's the matter with them hogs anyway?" a passing stranger asked.

"There ain't nothing the matter with them," the old farmer whispered hoarsely. "Them hogs belongs to me and

> *before I lost my voice I used to call them to their feed. After I lost my voice I used to tap on this fence rail with my stick at feeding time."*
>
> *He paused and shook his head gravely. "And now," he added, "them cussed woodpeckers up in them trees has got them poor hogs plumb crazy!"*

Just conditioning! That's what is happening to humanity.

One of the disciples of Pavlov, the pioneer and developer of the theory of the conditioned reflex, was trying an experiment along the same lines. He bought a puppy and decided to condition him to stand up and bark for his food. He held the pup's food just out of reach, barked a few times, then set it on the floor before him. The idea was that the pup would associate standing up and barking with getting his food and learn to do so when hungry.

This went on for about a week, but the little dog failed to learn. After another week the man gave up the experiment and simply put the food down in front of the dog, but the pup refused to eat it. He was waiting for his master to stand and bark! Now he had become conditioned.

It is only a conditioning, it can be dropped. You just need a little meditativeness. Meditation simply means the process of unconditioning the mind. Whatever the society has done to you has to be undone. When you are unconditioned you will be able to see the beauty of love and freedom together; they are two aspects of the same coin. If you really love the person you will give him or her absolute freedom—that's a gift of love. And when there is freedom, love responds tremendously. When you give freedom to somebody you have given the greatest gift, and love comes rushing towards you.

You ask me: "Is this some stupid *Waiting for Godot* game I am playing with myself?" No.

"When the last love affair ended, I swore to myself I was not going to let the same old deadening process happen, but here I am again feeling half alive, waiting for 'him' to come." But just by making a vow, just by deciding, you cannot change yourself. You have to understand. Love is a basic need, as basic as freedom, so both have to be fulfilled. And a person who is full of love *and* free is the most beautiful phenomenon in the world. And when two persons of such beauty meet, their relationship is not a relationship at all. It is a relating. It is a constant, riverlike flow. It is continuously growing towards greater heights.

The ultimate height of love and freedom is the experience of the divine. In it you will find both tremendous love, absolute love, and absolute freedom.

?

I am always afraid of being alone, because when I am alone I start to wonder who I am. It feels that if I inquire deeper, I will find out that I am not the person who I have believed I was for the past twenty-six years, but a being, present at the moment of birth and maybe also the moment before. For some reason, this scares me completely. It feels like a kind of insanity, and makes me lose myself in outside things in order to feel safer. Who am I, and why the fear?

It is not only your fear, it is everybody's fear. Because nobody is what he was supposed to be by existence.

The society, the culture, the religion, the education have all been conspiring against innocent children. They have all the powers, the child is helpless and dependent. So whatsoever they want to make out of him, they manage to do it. They don't allow any child to grow to his natural destiny. Their every effort is to make human beings into utilities.

Who knows, if a child is left on his own to grow, whether he will be of any use to the vested interests or not? The society is not prepared to take the risk. It grabs the child and starts molding him into something that is needed by the society. In a certain sense, it kills the soul of the child and gives him a false identity, so that he never misses his soul, his being.

The false identity is a substitute. But that substitute is useful only in the same crowd which has given it to you. The moment you are alone, the false starts falling apart and the repressed real starts expressing itself.

Hence the fear of being lonely. Nobody wants to be lonely, everybody wants to belong to a crowd—not only one crowd, but many crowds. A person belongs to a religious crowd, a political party, a rotary club, and there are many other small groups to belong to. One wants to be supported twenty-four hours a day because the false, without support, cannot stand. The moment one is alone, one starts feeling a strange craziness.

That's what you have been asking about because for twenty-six years you believed yourself to be somebody, and then suddenly in a moment of being alone you start feeling you are not that. It creates fear; then who are you? And twenty-six years of suppression—it will take some time for the real to express itself. The gap between the two has been called by the mystics "the dark night of the soul"—a very appropriate expression. You are no more the false, and you are not yet the real. You are in a limbo, you don't know who you are.

Particularly in the West—and the questioner comes from the West—the problem is even more complicated. Because they have not developed any methodology to discover the real as soon as possible, so that the dark night of the soul can be shortened. The West knows nothing as far as meditation is concerned. And meditation is only a name for being alone, silent, waiting for the real to assert itself. It is not an act, it is a silent relaxation because whatever you do will come out of your false personality. All your doing for twenty-six years has come out of it; it is an old habit.

Habits die hard.

There was one great mystic in India, Eknath. He was going for a holy pilgrimage with all his disciples. It was almost three to six months' journey.

One man came to him, fell at his feet, and said, "I know I am not worthy. You know it too, everybody knows me. But I know your compassion is greater than my unworthiness. Please accept me also as one of the members of the group that is going on the holy pilgrimage."

Eknath said, "You are a thief, and not an ordinary thief, but a master thief. You have never been caught, and everybody knows that you are a thief. I certainly feel like taking you with me, but I also have to think about those fifty other people who are going with me. You will have to give me a promise—and I am not asking for more, just for these three to six months' time while we are on the pilgrimage: you will not steal. After that, it is up to you. Once we are back home, you are free from the promise."

The man said, "I am absolutely ready to promise, and I am tremendously grateful for your compassion."

The other fifty people were suspicious. To trust in a thief . . . , but they could not say anything to Eknath, he was the master.

The pilgrimage started, and from the very first night there was trouble. The next morning there was chaos: somebody's coat was missing, somebody's shirt was missing, somebody's money was gone. And everybody was shouting, "Where is my money?" and they were all telling Eknath, "We were worried from the very beginning that you were taking this man with you. A lifelong habit—."

But then they started looking, and they found that things were not stolen. Somebody's money was missing, but it was found in somebody else's bag. Somebody else's coat was missing, but it was found in somebody else's luggage. Everything was found, but it was an unnecessary trouble—every morning! And nobody could conceive what can be the meaning of it? Certainly it is not the thief, because nothing was actually stolen.

The third night, Eknath remained awake to see what was going on. In the middle of the night, the thief—just out of habit—woke up, started taking things from one place to another place. Eknath stopped him and said, "What are you doing? Have you forgotten your promise?"

He said, "No, I have not forgotten my promise. I am not stealing anything, but I have not promised that I will not move things from one place to another place. After six months I have to be a thief again; this is just practice. And you must understand, it is a lifelong habit, you cannot drop it just like that. Just give me time. You should understand my problem also. For three days I have not stolen a single thing—it is just like fasting! This is just a substitute, I am keeping myself busy. This is my business time, in the middle of the night, so it is very hard for me just to lie down on the bed awake. And so many idiots are sleeping and I am not doing any harm to anybody. In the morning they will find their things."

Eknath said, "You are a strange man. You see that every morning there is such chaos, and one or two hours unnecessarily are wasted in finding where you have put things, whose property has gone into whose luggage. Everybody has to open everything and ask everybody . . .'To whom does this belong?' "

The thief said, "This much concession you have to give to me."

Twenty-six years of a false personality imposed by people who you loved, whom you respected, and they were not intentionally doing anything bad to you. Their intentions were good, just their awareness was nil. They were not conscious people: your parents, your teachers, your priests, your politicians were not conscious people, they were unconscious. And even a good intention in the hands of an unconscious person turns out to be poisonous.

So whenever you are alone, a deep fear arises because suddenly the false starts disappearing. And the real will take a little time. You have lost it twenty-six years back. You will have to give some consideration to the fact that a gap of twenty-six years has to be bridged.

In fear that "I am losing myself, my senses, my sanity, my mind, everything," because the self that has been given to you by others consists of all these things—it looks like you will go insane. You immediately start doing something just to keep yourself engaged. If there are no people, at least there is some action. So the false remains engaged and does not start disappearing.

Hence, people find it the most difficult on holidays. For five days they work, hoping that on the weekend they are going to relax. But the weekend is the worst time in the whole world. More accidents happen on the weekend, more people commit suicide, more murders, more stealing, more rape. Strange, these people were engaged for five days and there was no problem. But the weekend suddenly gives them a choice, either to be engaged in something or to relax, but relaxing is fearsome; the false personality disappears. Keep engaged, do anything stupid.

People are running toward the beaches, bumper to bumper, miles-long traffic. And if you ask them where they are going, they are "getting away from the crowd" and the whole crowd is going with them! They are going to find a solitary, silent space—all of them. In fact, if they had remained home it would have been more solitary and silent, because all the idiots have gone in search of a solitary place. And they are rushing like mad, because two days will be finished soon, they have to reach don't ask where! And on the beaches, you can see. Not even marketplaces are so crowded.

Strangely enough, people are feeling very much at ease, taking a sunbath. Ten thousand people on a small beach taking a sunbath, relaxing.

The same person on the same beach alone will not be able to relax. But he knows thousands of other people are relaxing all around him. The same people were in the offices, the same people were in the streets, the same people were in the marketplace, now these people are on the beach.

The crowd is an essential for the false self to exist. The moment it is lonely, you start freaking out. This is where one should understand a little bit of meditation.

Don't be worried, because that which can disappear is worth disappearing. It is meaningless to cling to it—it is not yours, it is not you. You are the one when the false has gone and the fresh, the innocent, the unpolluted being will arise in its place.

Nobody else can answer your question "Who am I?"—you will know it.

All meditative techniques are a help to destroy the false. They don't give you the real—the real cannot be given. That which can be given cannot be real. The real you have got already; just the false has to be taken away.

Meditation is just a courage to be silent and alone. Slowly, you start feeling a new quality to yourself, a new aliveness, a new beauty, a new intelligence, which is not borrowed from anybody, which is growing within you. It has roots in your existence. And if you are not a coward, it will come to fruition, to flowering.

Only the brave, the courageous, the people who have guts can be religious. Not the churchgoers: these are the cowards. Not the Hindus, not the Mohammedans, not the Christians: they are against searching. It is the same crowd, and they are trying to make their false identity more consolidated.

You were born. You have come into the world with life, with

consciousness, with tremendous sensitivity. Just look at a small child. Look at his eyes, the freshness. All that has been covered by a false personality.

There is no need to be afraid. You can lose only that which needs to be lost. And it is good to lose it soon, because the longer it stays, the stronger it becomes, and one does not know anything about tomorrow. Don't die before realizing your authentic being. Only those few people are fortunate who have lived with authentic being and who have died with authentic being because they know that life is eternal, and death is a fiction.

Then move out of it! One should always be watchful, because if one is not feeling happy in any situation, in any mood, then one should come out of it. Otherwise that becomes your habit, and by and by you lose sensitivity. You will go on being miserable and living in it, which simply shows a very deep insensitivity.

There is no need! If you are not feeling good in isolation, then come out of it. Meet with people, enjoy company, talk and laugh, but when you feel you are fed up with it, move into isolation again.

Always remember to judge everything by your inner feeling of bliss. If you are feeling blissful, everything is all right. If you are not feeling blissful, then whatsoever you are doing, something somewhere is wrong. The longer you remain in it, the more it becomes just an unaware thing, and you completely forget that it is through your cooperation that the miserable feeling continues. It needs your cooperation; it cannot exist itself.

Human growth requires that one moves from one polarity to another. Sometimes being alone is perfectly good: one needs one's own space, one needs to forget the whole world, and to be oneself. The other is absent so you have no boundary to yourself. The other creates your boundary, otherwise you are infinite.

Living with people, moving in the world, in society, by and by one begins to feel confined, limited, as if there are walls all around.

It becomes a subtle imprisonment, and one needs to move. One needs sometimes to be perfectly alone so that all boundaries disappear, as if the other does not exist at all, and the whole universe and the whole sky exists only for you. In that moment of aloneness one realizes for the first time what infinity is.

But then if you live in it too much, by and by the infinity bores you, it becomes tasteless. There is purity and silence, but there is no ecstasy in it. Ecstasy always comes through the other. One then starts feeling hungry for love, and wants to escape from this aloneness, this vast expanse of space. One wants a cozy place surrounded by others, so that one can forget oneself.

This is the basic polarity of life, love and meditation. People who try to live through love and relationships alone, by and by become very limited. They lose infinity and purity, and they become superficial. Always living in relationships means always living on the boundary where you can meet the other. So you are always standing at the gate, and you can never move into your palace, because only at the gate is the meeting-point where the other passes by. So people who only live in love, by and by become superficial. Their life loses depth. And people who live only in meditation will become very deep, but their life loses color, loses the ecstatic dance, the orgasmic quality of being.

Real humanity, the humanity of the future, will live with both the polarities together, and to share that understanding is my whole effort. One should be free to move from one to another, with neither polarity becoming a confinement. You should not be afraid of the marketplace, nor too afraid of the monastery. You should be free to move from the marketplace to the monastery, and from the monastery to the marketplace.

This freedom, this flexibility of movement, I call *sannyas*. The bigger the swing, the richer your life. There are attractions to remaining with just one of the polarities because then life is simpler. If you just remain with people, in the crowd, it is simple.

Complexity comes with the contradictory, the opposite pole. If you become a monk or you go to the Himalayas and just live there, life is very simple. But a simple life which has no complexity in it loses much richness.

Life should be both complex and simple. One has to seek this harmony continuously; otherwise life becomes of one note, a single note. You can go on repeating it, but no orchestra can be created out of it.

So whenever you feel that something is now becoming troublesome, immediately move before you become unaware. Never make anywhere your home, neither relationships nor aloneness. Remain flowing and homeless, and don't abide at any polarity. Enjoy it, delight in it, but when it is finished move to the other: make it a rhythm.

You work in the day, by night you rest, so that again by the next day you are ready to work, energy regained. Just think of a man who goes on working all day and all night, or who goes on sleeping day and night—what kind of a life will that be? One will be a madness, the other a coma. Between the two there is a balance, a harmony. Work hard so that you can relax. Relax deeply so that you become capable of working, of being more creative.

?

Please help me! My boyfriend has been in Goa for five weeks and I've had such a good time enjoying the freedom and independence, no need to face my jealousy and possessiveness, just floating through the day. Now it looks as if he is coming back soon and I'm getting nervous already, wondering what he is doing, how it is going to be, if he found somebody else, et cetera. What is this attachment to a particular person which creates all these comfortable and very uncomfortable feelings?

I'm not really a meditative type, but is there any possibility to go beyond this attachment of the heart and feel free, or is the only way to live it, go through it, and suffer and enjoy the whole thing?

I know your boyfriend: he will make anybody happy if he goes to Goa and remains there forever! He is a challenge, so if you are becoming nervous, it is natural. And don't be worried about his getting involved with any girl, because no girl will get involved with him.

I have thought about him and I think that only you can manage him. He's a crackpot but you love him. You cannot love a simple human being. You are born for each other: neither can you find another boyfriend nor can he find another girlfriend. So don't be worried about possessiveness or anything. You can be absolutely non-possessive, still he will be your boyfriend. Where else can he go? You are in a good, secured, guaranteed, insured condition.

In the first place, it is a miracle that you have found him. When I heard about it for the first time I said, "My God! Now something mysterious is going to happen. These two people together are going to create so much trouble." But still, he's attached to you, you are attached to him. Mostly your love is fighting, and when you are tired of fighting you love also, but that is only when you are both tired. He will also be feeling nervous, because he has to come back. I had suggested to him that he go away for a few weeks. He left immediately, the very moment he received my message: "Go to Goa." He did not wait even a single day! He must have enjoyed those five weeks the same way you have enjoyed them. Now you are feeling nervous, and he will be feeling nervous because those weeks will finally come to an end.

But deep down you are also feeling happy that he is coming

back, and the same will be his situation. Let him come. He's just your old boyfriend: you know him every bit, he knows you every bit. All the fights are well known, all the problems are well known. There is no need to feel nervous because there is not going to be anything new. It is just the same old chap, so let him come back and start life again in the same old way.

It is something to be understood: the girlfriend you get or the boyfriend you get, you deserve. You don't get any boyfriend or girlfriend whom you don't deserve; those kinds of relationships only last for one or two days. But your relationship has a history and it is going to last to the very end, so relax and take it easily!

You deserve him, he deserves you. And once you see the point that you deserve each other there is no question of any grudge, any complaining, any grumbling. You are strong enough, because that crackpot has not been able to make even a dent in you. He has been doing all kinds of neurotic things. But he does not know that you are a psychotic, and neurotics and psychotics make good marriages. They fit perfectly.

One psychoanalyst was asked—because those two words look so similar, and the difference is known only to the experts—the psychoanalyst was asked, "What is the difference between neurosis and psychosis?"

He said, "The psychotic thinks two plus two are five and, whatever you do, he never changes his mind. He's determined and committed to his viewpoint. The neurotic knows that two plus two are four but feels very nervous—why are they four?"

Perfect marriages happen only in heaven, but once in a while on the earth too. You and your boyfriend are a perfect combination. So let the poor fellow come, start hammering each other in the old way. You are accustomed and well trained, he is accustomed and well trained. One feels worried about a new girlfriend; one never knows what she is going to do—freak out in the middle of the night? One is nervous about the new boyfriend, because one cannot predict what kind of man he's going to prove to be.

You are certain. In this certainty you should relax and let him come. I don't see that there is any problem. You are both perfectly happy in your misery; all people are perfectly happy in their miserable relationships! That's why after a five weeks' separation you feel good. If the separation is for a longer time you will start missing him.

I have given just enough time so that you can enjoy freedom and he can enjoy freedom, and in the right moment, when you start missing each other, he's back. Just wait!

And he's not a dangerous person; he cannot harm you. He's very good at heart, just a little loose in his head. But to have a boyfriend who is a little loose in the head is better than to have a boyfriend who is a little tight in the head. I know it is no ordinary relationship: you both are extraordinary.

SOUL MATES OR CELL MATES?

We are all living lives according to fictions, poetries, film stories. That has given humanity a wrong impression, the impression that when there is love everything will fit, that there will be no conflict. For centuries poets have been giving the idea that lovers are made for each other.

Nobody is made for anybody else. Everybody is different from everybody else. You may love a person without knowing that you love the person only because there is so much difference between you, so much distance. The distance is a challenge, the distance is an adventure; the distance makes the woman or the man worth getting hold of. But things as they appear from a distance are not the same when they come close.

When you are just courting a man or a woman, everything is beautiful, everything fits because both want everything to fit. Anything that does not fit is not allowed to surface; it is repressed in the unconscious. So lovers sitting on the beach looking at the moon do not know each other at all. The marriage is almost finished before the honeymoon is finished.

In the East where the tradition of arranged marriage is still followed, there is nothing like a honeymoon; they don't give the chance for the marriage to be finished so soon. Couples go on living together and never feel that things are not fitting, that something is missing. There is no chance at all for that to happen. Husbands and wives do not choose for themselves; marriages are organized by the parents, by the astrologers, by all kinds of people except the two who are going to be married.

Even after they get married, the couple cannot see each other alone in the daylight, they can only meet each other deep in the darkness of the night. They live with their families, and those families are so big that they can talk only in whispers; fighting is out of the question. Throwing clothes will not work; no woman, no man in these traditional communities knows that clothes have to be thrown, otherwise what kind of love affair do you have? Or that plates have to be broken, or that you have to argue over each and every thing. You say one thing and the woman understands something else; she says something, you understand something else.

But in the modern marriages based on love affairs, there seems to be no communication. And it starts with the honeymoon, because there for the first time you are together twenty-four hours a day. Now you cannot pretend; you have to be real. You cannot act. When you live together you have to be real to the other person; you cannot hide, you cannot have any secrets. And we have been given the idea from our very childhood that between wife and husband there is always harmony, everything is always fitting, they are always together, always loving, no fight. That whole ideology is the problem.

I would like to tell you the truth. The truth is that both the persons, whoever they are, are different individuals. If you love somebody you have to understand that the person you love is not your shadow, is not your reflection in the mirror, has his or her own individuality. Unless you have a big enough heart to accommodate somebody who is different from you, who may have different ideas about different things, you should not get into unnecessary trouble. It is better to become a monk or a nun. Why bother? Why create hell for yourself and the other?

But the hell is created because you expect heaven.

I am telling you to accept that this is the situation: the person is going to be different. You are not the master, neither is the other the master; both are simply partners who have decided, in spite of all differences, to be together. And in fact, differences add spice to your love. If you can find a person who is just like you, you will not find much attraction. The other person has to be different, distant, a mystery that invites you to explore.

With two mysteries meeting together, once they drop the idea that they have to agree on everything, there is no question of any fight. The fight arises because you want agreement.

If you are living just like two friends, she has her own ideas, you have your own ideas, she respects your ideas, you respect her ideas; she has her way, you have your own way and nobody is trying to impose on and indoctrinate the other. Then there is no question of fight. And then there is no question that things are not fitting. Why should they be fitting?

Why should there be any feeling that something is missing? Nothing is missing; it is just that your idea of harmony is not there. Harmony is not something very great, it is boring. Once in a while, even if you fight, once in a while even if you get really hot, that does not mean that love disappears; that simply means love is capable of absorbing even disagreements, fights, overcoming all these hindrances. But the old ideology gets in the way of your understanding.

I am reminded of the old biblical story which is not told very much because it is very dangerous. First, God made one man and one woman. But as you know by looking at the world, God does not seem to be very intelligent. Here, nothing is fitting; from the very beginning you can see it. He made man and woman, two persons, and gave them a small bed, not a double bed.

The very first night, at the beginning of time, was the night of a tremendous fight because the woman wanted to sleep on the bed. The man thought that he should sleep on the bed and she should sleep on the floor. The whole night they went on fighting, hitting each other, throwing things, and in the morning the man said to God, "I asked you to give me a companion but I did not ask you to give me an enemy. If this is your idea of a companion, then I want to tell you I was better off alone. I don't want this woman; there is never going to be peace between us."

Now the simple thing would have been to ask for a double bed. I don't understand what kind of God that was, and what these idiots were asking. The simple solution was a double bed, or two single beds, if things were getting that bad. But instead of that Adam said, "I don't want this woman; she is trying to be equal to me." The male chauvinist idea arose that very night.

So God dismantled the woman—naturally, because God is also a male chauvinist. Her name was Lilith. He dismantled her just the way you dismantle any mechanism. He destroyed the woman and said, "Now I will make another woman who will be lower than you and will never ask for equality." Then he made the second woman, who was Eve, by taking one of the ribs from Adam. Out of Adam's rib he made the woman, so that she could ask for equality; she was nothing but a rib.

It is said that every night when Adam would come back home and go to sleep, Eve would count his ribs because she was always afraid that if he lost anther rib, that would mean another woman was also somewhere around.

There is no need for more than friendship. Love has to be a friendly affair in which nobody is superior, in which nobody is going to decide about things, in which both are fully aware that they are different, that their approach towards life is different, that they think differently, and still, with all these differences, they love each other.

Then you will not find any problems. Problems are created by us.

Don't try to create something superhuman. Be human, accept the other person's humanity with all the frailty humanity is prone to. Your partner will commit mistakes just as you commit mistakes, and you have to learn. To be together is a great learning: of forgiving, forgetting, understanding that the other is as human as you are. Just a little forgiveness.

There is an old proverb: "To err is human and to forgive is divine." I don't agree. To err is human and to forgive is also human. To forgive is divine?—then you are raising it too high, beyond human reach. Bring it within human reach and learn to forgive. Learn to enjoy forgiveness, learn to offer an apology; you don't lose anything when you can say to your partner, "I'm sorry, I was wrong."

But nobody wants to say, "I was wrong." You want to be always right. The man tries to prove through arguments that he is right, and the woman tries through emotions to prove that she is right—screaming, crying, weeping, tears. And most often she wins! The man becomes afraid of the neighbors, and just to cool her down—because the children may wake up—he says, "Cool down, perhaps you are right." But deep down he still believes he is right.

To be understanding means that you can be wrong, the woman may be right. It is not a guarantee that just by being man you have the power and authority to be right; neither has the woman. If we were just a little more human and a little more friendly, and we could say to each other, "I am sorry." And what are the things you are fighting for? So small, so trivial that if somebody asks you to tell them about it you will feel embarrassed.

Just drop the idea that everything has to fit, drop the idea that there is going to be total harmony because those are not good ideas. If everything fits you will get bored with each other; if everything is harmonious you will lose the whole juice of the relationship. It is good that things don't fit. It is good that there is always a gap so there is always something to explore, something to cross over, some bridge to be made. The whole life can be a tremendous exploration of each other if we accept the differences, the basic uniqueness of each individual, and we make love not a kind of slavery but a friendship.

Try friendship, try friendliness; and remember always, there is nothing that is going to disturb you. When you see a beautiful woman, you feel attracted; you should understand that when your wife sees a beautiful man, she must be feeling attracted. If you are understanding, you will both discuss, lovingly, what a beautiful woman she was, and what a beautiful man he was.

But right now the situation is that you can see from miles away whether the couple coming is married or unmarried. With the married couple, the husband moves very cautiously and very carefully; he does not look here and there, as if he has got some neck problem. And the wife is watching where he is looking, what he is looking at, and taking note of everything. This is ugly.

I was traveling—I was going to Kashmir—and in my compartment there was a beautiful woman. Her husband was coming to her at every station with ice cream, and with bananas, apples. In Kashmir, the fruits are really good.

I asked the woman, "How long have you been married?"

She said, "Seven years."

I said, "Don't lie to me."

She said, "What do you mean? Why should I lie to you?"

I said, "This man has been coming to you at every station and bringing all these things. So it's clear to me that he is not your husband."

She said, "How did you come to know?"

I said, "If he was your husband, especially if you had been married seven years, then once he had dropped you off in this compartment, only at the last stop—if you were fortunate—would he come back to get you; for the rest of the journey he would be gone. Why should he come to you at every station with all these treats?"

She said, "Strange, but you are right. He is not my husband; he is a friend's husband, but he loves me. And what you are saying about husbands is true. That has happened between me and my husband. We live together but we are miles apart; I am thinking to divorce him."

I said, "Don't do that. Go on living with him and go on loving this man, and don't let this man divorce his wife. She is probably already seeing somebody else, so don't be worried. Existence takes care of things. But if you divorce your husband and get married to this man, you will not get these ice creams and fruits and all this attention and love; all of that will disappear."

If you are just friendly and don't make your friendliness a legal affair of husband and wife, things will be far better because then you are not a burden to anybody, not a bondage. There will be no question of having to fit with each other. You can have your individuality totally free from each other, and yet be in love.

And really to be totally different in your individuality creates the best possibility of love.

Whenever I am in love with a man, for that time no other man attracts me. But for the man, it's not the same. Though he is happy and satisfied, and wants to keep the relationship with me, he has his short love affairs every few months. I understand the different nature of man and woman. I also understand every love relationship has its peaks and valleys. Still, sadness in me keeps on coming. I give a long rope to the man. My friends say I make myself so available that I let the man take me for granted and I lose my self-respect. I'm not clear. I don't expect anything from him. Would you please like to comment?

There are many things in your question. First, you have a misunderstanding about man's nature. You think, as many people in the world think, that a man is polygamous and a woman is monogamous, that the woman wants to live with one man, to love one man, to devote and dedicate herself totally to one man, but man is different in nature. He wants to love other women too, at least once in a while.

The reality is that both are polygamous. The woman has been conditioned by man for thousands of years into thinking that she is monogamous. And man is very cunning; he has exploited the woman in many ways. One of the ways is that he has been telling her that men are, by nature, polygamous. All the psychologists, all the sociologists are agreed upon the fact that men are polygamous, and none of them says the same thing about women.

My own understanding is that both are polygamous. If a

woman does not behave in a polygamous way, it is nurture, not nature. She has been utterly conditioned so long that the conditioning has gone into her very blood, into her bones, into her very marrow. For centuries the woman had to depend financially on the man, and the man has cut her wings, he has curtailed her freedom, he has undermined her dependence upon herself. He has taken her responsibilities on his shoulders, showing great love, saying, "You need not be worried about yourself, I will take care." But in the name of love, he has taken the freedom of the woman. For centuries women were not allowed to be educated, to be qualified in any way in any craft, in any skill; she had to be financially dependent on the man. He has taken away even her freedom of movement; she could not move freely the way man moves; she was confined to the house. The house was almost her imprisonment.

And in the past particularly, she was always pregnant because out of ten children, nine children used to die. To have two or three living children a woman had to be continually pregnant the whole time she was capable of reproducing. A pregnant woman becomes even more dependent financially, the man becomes her caretaker. The man was knowledgeable, the woman knew nothing. She was kept ignorant because knowledge is power; that's why women were deprived of knowledge. And because it has been a man's world, they all agreed as far as keeping the woman enslaved was concerned.

She has been told that it is her nature to be monogamous. There was not a single psychoanalyst, not a single woman sociologist to refute this and ask, if man is polygamous then why should woman be monogamous? Man made the way for his polygamy by creating prostitutes. It was an accepted fact in the past that no wife would have objected if her husband, once in a while, visited a prostitute. It was thought that it is just natural for man.

I say to you that both are polygamous. The whole existence is polygamous, it has to be so—monogamy is boredom. However beautiful a woman may be, however beautiful a man may be, you become tired—the same geography, the same topography. How long do you have to see the same face? So it happens that years pass, and the husband has not looked attentively at his wife for a single moment.

In the new world, there should be no marriage, only lovers. And as long as they are pleased to be together, they can be together; and the moment they feel that they have been together too long, a little change will be good. There is no question of sadness, no question of anger, just a deep acceptance of nature. And if you have loved a man or a woman, you will want to give the other person as much freedom as possible.

If love cannot give freedom, then it is not love.

You say, "Sadness in me keeps on coming. I give a long rope to the man." Now, the very idea is wrong. Is your man a dog that you give him a long rope? You cannot give freedom, freedom is everybody's birthright. The very idea, "I'm giving a long rope"—still the rope is in your hand! You are the giver of freedom.

You cannot give freedom; you can only accept the freedom of the other person. You cannot keep one end of the rope in your hand, watching the dog pissing on this tree, pissing on that tree. You think that is freedom? No, the very idea is wrong. The other person has his freedom; you have your freedom. Neither does he need to have one end of the rope in his hand, nor do you; otherwise, both are chained. His rope is going to be your chains, your rope is going to be his chains. And you think you give "enough rope." You think you are being very generous!

Freedom is not something that has to be given to another person. Freedom is something that has to be recognized as the birthright of the other person.

The freedom of a person you love will not hurt you. It hurts because you don't use your own freedom. It is not his freedom that hurts; what hurts is that you have been incapacitated by centuries of wrong conditioning—you cannot use your own freedom. Man has taken your whole freedom, that is the real problem. Your freedom has to be returned to you, and it will not hurt; in fact you will enjoy it.

Freedom is such a joyful experience. Your lover is enjoying freedom, you are enjoying freedom; in freedom you meet, in freedom you part. And perhaps life may bring you together again.

When your man becomes interested in another woman, it does not mean that he no longer loves you; it simply means just a change of taste. Once in a while, you like to go to the pizza place. That does not mean that you have renounced your old food, but once in a while, it is perfectly good. In fact, after visiting the pizza place, you go back to your own table more joyously. It takes a few days for you to forget the experience, and then again one day you again want pizza. These affairs don't mean much. One cannot live on pizza alone.

Couples who love each other should have a few love affairs once in a while. Those love affairs will renew their relationship, will refresh it. You will start seeing beauty again in your wife. You may start fantasies, dreams of having your wife again. You will realize that you misunderstood her before; this time you are not going to misunderstand. And the same is true about your husband.

In my idea of a loving community, people will be absolutely free to say to their partner: "I would like two days holiday, and you are also free; you need not sit in the house and boil." If you want to meditate, that is another thing; otherwise you have been interested in the neighbor's wife too long. The green grass on the other side of the fence—you wanted to explore it for so long, now your wife is giving you a chance! You should say, "You are great! Just go for a holiday and enjoy it. And I'm going to the neighbor's house, the grass is greener there." But in two days, you will find that grass is grass, and your own lawn was far better.

But an authentic experience is needed, and when after two days, you meet again it will be the beginning of a new honeymoon. Why not have honeymoons every month? Why be satisfied with one honeymoon in one life? That is strange, and absolutely unnatural. And love is not something bad or evil so that you have to prevent your wife loving somebody else. It is just fun; there is not much to be bothered about. If she wants to play tennis with somebody, let her play! I don't think that making love has more significance than playing tennis. In fact, tennis is far cleaner.

You say, "I don't expect anything from him." Even in your no-expectations, there are hidden expectations unspoken. And they are more subtle, and more binding. Simply, one has to accept a simple fact: your partner is a stranger; it is just an accident that you are together and you never expect anything from strangers.

Love as much as you can. Never think of the next moment; and if your lover goes somewhere else, you are also free. And don't deceive yourself; can any woman say that while she is in love with one person, she does not get attracted to other people? Maybe it is a repressed desire, maybe she never allows it to surface; but it is impossible not to, because there are so many beautiful people around. You have chosen only one stranger amongst many strangers.

Keep freedom as a higher value than love itself. And if it is possible—and it is possible because it is natural—your life will not be a misery. It will be a continuous excitement, a continuous exploration of new human beings. We are all strangers: nobody is a husband, nobody is a wife. Some idiot registrar cannot, just by putting his seal on a paper, make you a husband and wife. And once that man has put the seal, if you want to separate you have to go to another idiot—bigger idiots—and wait for months or years to be separated. Strange! It is your private affair; it is no business of any registrar, no business of any judge. Why do you go on giving your freedom to the hands of others?

You say, "My friends say I make myself so available that I let the man take me for granted, and I lose my self-respect." Your friends don't understand a thing and they are not your friends either because their advice is that of enemies.

One should make oneself absolutely available. Your friends are telling you that when your man wants to make love to you, one day you should say you have a headache. Another day, you should say you are too tired; the third day, you are not in the mood. Keep the man hanging around. "Don't give that much rope"—just a little rope, and a beautiful bell around his neck with your name written on it, saying, "Beware, personal property."

What do you mean by "availability?" You should be available to the person you love, and if once in a while he feels to change, enjoy and let him go joyously. That will bring self-respect to you, and dignity.

A divorced woman, frustrated with married life, ran an ad in the local newspaper that read, "Looking for a man who won't beat me, who won't run around on me, and who is a fantastic lover."

After one week, her doorbell rings. She goes to the door, opens it, and sees no one there. She closes the door, and is about to walk away when the bell rings again.

Opening the door once again, she sees no one there, but happens to look down and notices a man with no arms and no legs sitting on the doorstep.

"I'm here to answer your ad," he says.

The woman does not know quite what to do, what to say.

So the man continues, "As you can see, I can't beat you, and it will be impossible for me to run around on you."

"Yes, I can see that," said the woman, "but the ad also said I wanted a 'fantastic lover.'"

The man smiles and says, "I rang the doorbell, didn't I?"

?

Although I am deeply satisfied and nourished by my regular food, still from time to time I feel a strong pull towards other dishes, and enjoy Italian pizzas, French wine, or Japanese sushi. It's not that I don't want to eat out occasionally, but I'd like to feel it is in my hands whether I do or not, and not be a victim of this hormonal conspiracy. Can you please give me a clue how to go beyond these biological pulls?

If one allows nature without any inhibitions to take its own course, one transcends biology, body, mind, without any effort. But we are full of inhibitions. Even the so-called young people, who think that they have disowned repressions, are in a very subtle way repressive. If you are repressive then you cannot transcend biological pulls naturally, without any effort. So, the first thing to be remembered is that nature is right.

All the old traditions have been telling you that nature is not right. You have to divide nature into right and wrong. But nature is indivisible. So while you are dividing it, you are simply making an impossible effort. The whole of nature has to be accepted with great joy and gratitude. Biology is not your bondage, but a certain stage of growth.

Life taken with insight and understanding helps you to go beyond itself without asking you for any discipline, any effort, any arduous conflict. We are children of nature. But all the religions have created one thing certainly: a divided mind, a schizophrenic man who is pulled in two directions. They have all given you moralities.

The natural man needs no morality. Easy is right. To be natural, to be spontaneous is right and transcendence comes on its own. The people who are split against themselves—that biology is something to be transcended, that body is something to be fought, that mind is something to be dropped—anybody who is entangled in all these conflicts will never transcend.

One should go more easily. It is not a war field. Your life is an autonomous growth. The first need is of a total acceptance with no reluctance, no unwillingness, no subtle condemnation anywhere in your mind.

You are saying, "Although I am deeply satisfied and nourished by my regular food. . . ." You say you are deeply satisfied, but you don't understand the nuances of being deeply satisfied. It becomes a kind of death. To be alive one needs a little discontent, a little restlessness. If you are deeply satisfied, from that deep satisfaction arises your desire to change your food once in a while.

Man is a creature of evolution and growth. Being deeply satisfied brings a full stop to your life. Your partner has an individuality, a grace, a loving heart, and it is very easy to be satisfied with her; she is not a quarreling type, a fighting type. She herself is at ease, and anybody who loves her will find himself soon at ease. A harmony arises but harmony on the one hand is beautiful, and on the other hand is boring.

Perhaps you have never thought that satisfaction is a kind of death. It means you are ready to repeat the same every day, that you have forgotten to change, to evolve.

". . . Still from time to time I feel a strong pull towards other dishes, and enjoy Italian pizzas, French wine, or Japanese sushi." It is absolutely natural. The problem is arising because of your conditionings that when you are absolutely satisfied with a woman, why should you ask? Why should the desire for somebody else even arise in you? It arises because of your deep satisfaction. Deep satisfaction starts deadening you; nothing new, no excitement, no possibility of "No," always "Yes." On the one hand it is very sweet; on the other, it is *too* sweet.

Hence, the desire arises once in a while to have some affair with another woman. It is absolutely natural. If your partner were a fighting type, nagging type, bitchy, this desire would not have arisen so much because she would never have allowed you to be satisfied. She would have kept you always unsatisfied; she would have remained a stranger to you, still to be explored. I know her. She has been open to you, available to you; she has not been holding secrets from you. That is not her fault, that is her beauty. But even the most beautiful rose flowers have their thorns, even the most satisfying situations have their problems.

Because you are too satisfied, you start asking for a change of taste: Italian pizzas, French wine, or Japanese sushi. Nothing is wrong in it. The whole old conditioning goes against what I am saying to you, but if you are intelligent, you will see the point.

Accept it, but don't keep it a secret from your lover. Don't let her down. Don't make her feel that she is not enough for you. Say to her, "You are too satisfying, and my mind wants a little change of atmosphere, some excitement so that I can feel that I am still alive." And remember, whatever you take for yourself, you have to give her too. It has not to be one-sided, not that only you go to the pizza place, or find a Chinese restaurant; you allow her also. Not only allow. The woman has been repressed by man so much that you will have to pull her out from her conditionings. You will have to help her to move, once in a while, into new pastures. If you can do that you will not only be accepting your nature; you will also be helping her to find out her nature.

As a man, you are also guilty because it is the man who has forced the woman, made her monogamous. In fact, she needs to move with other people more than you do. The most astounding research about men and women is that a man can have only one orgasm, the woman can have multiple orgasms. The reason is simple: because in orgasm, a man loses energy, he will need to recover for some time, according to his age, to have another orgasm.

But the woman does not lose any energy. On the contrary, her first orgasm gives her a deep incentive to have more orgasms, and she is capable of at least half a dozen orgasms in a single night.

Because of this fact, man became so afraid that he prevented the woman from knowing the fact that anything like orgasm exists. So he is very quick in making love. The woman will take a little longer time: man's sexuality is local, genital; woman's sexuality is spread all over her body. If a man wants her to have an orgasm he has to play with her whole body, the foreplay, so her whole body starts throbbing with energy.

But once she has had one orgasm, she knows the taste, and she knows that now she can have deeper orgasms. But the man is simply impotent after the first orgasm, at least for a few hours. He cannot do anything else, he just turns over and goes to sleep. The poor boy is finished. And every woman weeps, cries because she has not even come and her lover is finished!

To prevent the woman from having the knowledge of orgasm—for centuries the woman was not allowed even to know the beauty and the pleasure of orgasm—man also has had to prevent himself from having orgasm. All that he knows is ejaculation; ejaculation is not orgasm. Ejaculation is simply throwing out energy: one feels more relaxed, the tensions of the energy are gone, and one snores better.

The woman has become aware of orgasm only in the last century and the whole credit goes to the movement of psychoanalysis. In the more traditional Eastern countries, 98 percent of women are still unaware that there is anything in making love, because she gets no juice, no experience. She in fact hates the whole affair. Ejaculation is not her need, it is man's need; but both have remained deprived of sex and its ultimate orgasmic experiences.

But the trouble is, how to manage it? Anything looks very immoral. Either you have to invite all your friends, so that five or six friends make love, one by one, to the woman. Then she will be satisfied, but that looks very hurting to the ego. Or you have to provide her with an electric vibrator. But once she knows the vibrator, you are useless because the vibrator gives her such tremendous orgasmic experiences that you cannot give.

It seems there has been some mistake by nature itself: men and women are not equal in their orgasmic capacity. You are fully satisfied, but have you ever bothered whether your beloved has found even a single orgasm? Because she has not found a single orgasm, she can remain devoted to you, monogamous. But if she knows what orgasmic experience is, she will also want, once in a while, to be with another man.

If you really love your woman, you will help her to come out of her old conditionings, which are far deeper, because man himself is responsible. Man himself does not have those conditionings; his morality is very superficial and a hypocrisy. But the woman's morality has gone very deep. Man has been enforcing it from the very childhood. If you feel to change it, it is your responsibility; and particularly a man of your understanding should be able to see what I am saying. It is your responsibility to bring Neelam also out into the sun, into the rain, into the wind, so that she can drop all her conditionings. You have to help her; you have to teach her how to enjoy the pizza place, and not go on eating the Punjabi food her whole life. How to enjoy Japanese food or Chinese food? If men and women really love each other, they will help each other to be unconditioned from the past.

Man does not have many conditionings, and they are superficial. He can drop them very easily, the way you drop your clothes. The woman has been conditioned so much that it is not like dropping her clothes, it is like peeling her skin. It is hard, and unless you really love a woman you will not be able to help her much. It will be very difficult, on her own, to get rid of all those conditionings, so help her. Give her also the taste that in the world there are so many other foods; there are many more beautiful men other than you. Your woman should know all of them. It is part of your love that your woman becomes more and more rich in her experiences. And the richer she is, she will not only give you satisfaction; she will start giving you excitement and ecstasy.

You say, "It's not that I don't want to eat out occasionally, but I'd like to feel it is in my hands whether I do or not. . . ." It is in your hands, but it can be in your hands only if it is in the hands of your partner, too. As far as I am concerned there should be equal opportunity for both. Not that you are the master and your woman is your slave; that she can remain satisfied with you, and you can go, once in a while, fooling around the neighborhood. She has every right to fool around in the same neighborhood! And there is no need to feel guilty; you have to help her not to feel guilty.

The woman's liberation will be the man's liberation, too; their slavery is together. Because you don't allow your woman to be free, how can she allow you to be free? Freedom has to be, from both sides, a precious value—loved, recognized, respected.

You say ". . . and not be a victim of this hormonal conspiracy." If you want to get beyond the hormones and the biology, live it totally, exhaust it.

My own understanding is that by the age of fourteen your hormones start working, and if you allow them total freedom, if you go with them joyously by the age forty-two, they will like to go to rest. And this transcendence will be natural; it will not be a celibacy imposed. It will be a sacred celibacy that is coming to you from the beyond, because you have lived your life totally and now nothing in the ordinary life interests you. Your interest is in higher values, for a deeper search about life, about truth, about creativity. You have passed a childish age. By the age of forty-two, according to me, a man really becomes adult, but only if he lives naturally. If he lives half-heartedly then it will take a longer time, maybe forty-nine years, maybe seventy-five. Maybe even when he is dying he is thinking only of sex and nothing else; he never transcends it.

You are both understanding people and can see things without screens on your eyes, clearly. Love each other totally, and occasionally allow each other freedom. But it has to be on both sides. And it is not going to destroy your love; it is going to make it richer, deeper, more fulfilling, more orgasmic. And those few occasions when you are on holiday from each other will not take you away from each other; they will go on bringing you closer to each other. Don't have any secret, be absolutely open, and allow the other person also to be absolutely open, and respect openness. Never, even by your gestures, make the other person feel guilty. That is the greatest crime humanity has been committing, making people guilty. If the other feels guilty because of very deep rooted conceptions, help her to be free of the guilt.

Love lived in an atmosphere of freedom will transcend sex naturally, easily, effortlessly. Love will remain, sex will be gone, and then love has a purity and a beauty and a sacredness of its own.

Sitting on a bus in New York, a prim old lady was shocked to overhear an Italian say to another, "Emma come-a first. I come-a next. Two ass-a come-a together. I come-a again. Two ass-a come-a together again. I come-a once more. Peepee twice. Then I come-a for the last time."

When the Italian was finished, the red-faced old maid turned to a policeman sitting nearby, and said, "Are you not going to arrest that terrible old man?"

"What for?" asked the policeman. "For spelling Mississippi?"

Take life more joyously and more jokingly. Let your whole life become a beautiful joke. There is nothing wrong in nature, and to be natural is to be religious.

You both are intelligent, and I hope that you will prove my hypothesis that you can love each other, and yet once in a while have different affairs—joyously, not reluctantly. Not because I am saying it, but out of your own understanding.

It doesn't seem like I'll ever be able to go beyond the biological, sexual attraction that you say is "lust" and grow into the kind of love you are talking about. How does it happen? Where do I start?

Sex is a subtle subject, delicate, because centuries of exploitation, corruption, centuries of perverted ideas and conditioning, are associated with the word "sex." The very word is loaded, it is one of the most loaded words in existence. You say "God" and it seems empty. You say "sex" and it seems too loaded. A thousand and one things arise in the mind: fear, perversion, attraction, a tremendous desire, and a tremendous anti-desire also. They all arise together. "Sex"—the very word creates confusion, chaos. It is as if somebody has thrown a rock in a silent pool, and millions of ripples arise just from the word! Humanity has lived under the influence of very wrong ideas.

So the first thing to consider is, why do you ask how to go beyond your sexual feelings? Why do you want in the first place to transcend your sexuality? You are using a beautiful term—"go beyond"—but out of a hundred possibilities, ninety-nine are that you mean, "How to repress my sexual feelings?"

A person who has understood that sex can be transcended is not even worried about going beyond it, because transcendence comes through experience. You cannot manage it. It is not something that you have to *do*. You simply pass through many experiences, and those experiences make you more and more mature.

Have you watched that at a certain age, sex becomes important?

Not that you make it important. It is not something that you *make* happen; it *happens*. At the age of fourteen, or somewhere near there, suddenly your energy is flooded with sex. It happens as if floodgates have been opened in you. Subtle sources of energy that were not open before have become open, and your whole energy becomes sexual, colored with sex. You think sex, you sing sex, you walk sex—everything becomes sexual. Every act is colored. This *happens;* you have not done anything about it. It is natural. And transcendence is also natural. If sex is lived totally, with no condemnation, with no idea of getting rid of it, then at the age of forty-two—just as at the age of fourteen the door to sex gets opened and the whole energy becomes sexual, at the age of forty-two or near about—those floodgates start to close again. And that too is as natural as sex becoming alive; it starts disappearing.

Sexuality is transcended not by any effort on your part. If you make any effort that will be repressive, because it has nothing to do with you. It is inbuilt—in your body, in your biology. You are born as sexual beings; nothing is wrong in it. That is the only way to be born. To be human is to be sexual. When you were conceived, your mother and your father were not praying, they were not listening to some priest's sermon. They were not in church, they were making love. Even to think that your mother and father were making love when you were conceived seems to be difficult, I know, but they were making love; their sexual energies were meeting and merging into each other. Then you were conceived; in that deep sexual act you were conceived. The first cell was a sexual cell, and then out of that cell other cells have arisen. But each cell remains sexual, basically. Your whole body is sexual, made of sex cells. Now they are millions.

Remember it: you exist as a sexual being. Once you accept it, the conflict that has been created down through the centuries starts to dissolve. Once you accept it deeply, with no ideas in between, when sex is thought of as simply natural, then you *live* it. You don't ask how to go beyond eating, you don't ask how to transcend breathing, because no religion has taught you to transcend breathing. That's why; otherwise you would be asking, "How to go beyond breathing?" But you don't ask, you simply breathe! You are a breathing animal. You are a sexual animal, also. But there is a difference. Fourteen years of your life, in the beginning, are almost non-sexual, or at the most there is just rudimentary sexual play, which is not really sexual—just preparing, rehearsing, that's all. By the age of fourteen, the energy is ripe.

Watch: a child is born and immediately, within just a few seconds, the child has to breathe; otherwise he will die. Then breathing remains for the whole of life, because it has come at the very first step of life. It cannot be transcended. Maybe before you die, then, just a few seconds before, it will stop, but not before that.

Always remember it: both ends of life, the beginning and end, are symmetrical. The child is born, he starts breathing within a matter of seconds. When the person is old and dying, the moment he stops breathing, within a matter of seconds he will be dead.

Sex enters at a relatively late stage: For twelve, fourteen years the child has lived without sex. And if the society is not too repressed and hence obsessed with sex, a child can live completely oblivious to the fact that sex, or anything like sex, exists. The child can remain absolutely innocent. That innocence is also not possible nowadays, because people are so repressed. When repression happens, then side by side obsession also happens. On the one side there are priests, who go on condemning sex, and then there are anti-priests, like Hugh Hefner and others, who go on making sexuality more and more glamorous. The priest and Hugh Hefner exist together as two sides of the same coin. When churches disappear, only then *Playboy* magazines will disappear, not before. They are partners in the same business! They look like enemies, but don't be deceived by that. They talk against each other, but that's how things work.

I have heard about two men who went out of business, they had gone broke, so they decided on a new and very simple business. They started traveling from one town to another. First one would enter, and in the night he would throw coal tar on people's windows and doors. After two or three days the second man would come to the same town. He would advertise that he could clean any kind of dirt from the outside of people's homes, even coal tar, and people all over town would hire him. During that time the other would be doing his half of the business in another town. This way, they started earning lots of money.

This is what is happening between the church and the people who are creating pornography.

I have heard:

> *Pretty Miss Keenan sat in the confessional. "Father," she said, "I want to confess that I let my boyfriend kiss me."*
>
> *"Is that all you did?" asked the priest, very interested.*
>
> *"Well, no. I let him put his hand on my leg, too."*
>
> *"And then what?"*
>
> *"And then I let him pull down my panties."*
>
> *"And then, and then . . . ?" questioned the priest, panting with excitement.*
>
> *"And then my mother walked into the room."*
>
> *"Ah, shit," sighed the priest.*

It is together; they are partners in a conspiracy. Whenever you are too repressed, you start finding a perverse interest. A perverted interest is the problem, not sex. Now this priest is neurotic. Sex is not the problem, but this man is in trouble.

Sisters Margaret Alice and Francis Catherine were out walking along a side street. Suddenly they were grabbed by two men, dragged into a dark alley, and raped. "Father, forgive them," said Sister Margaret Alice, "for they know not what they do."

"Shut up!" cried Sister Catherine, "this one does."

This is bound to be the situation. So never carry a single idea against sex in your mind, otherwise you will never be able to go beyond it into love. The only people who can go beyond "mere biological sexual attraction" are those who accept sex very naturally. It is difficult, I know, because you are born in a society that is neurotic about sex. Either condemning it or glamorizing it, but it is neurotic all the same. It is very difficult to get out of this neurosis, but if you are a little alert you can get out of it.

So the real thing is not how to transcend sex, but how to transcend this perverted ideology of the society—this fear of sex, this repression of sex, this obsession with sex.

Sex is beautiful. Sex in itself is a natural, rhythmic phenomenon. It happens when the child is ready to be conceived, and it is good that it happens; otherwise life would not exist. Life exists through sex; sex is its medium. If you understand life, if you love life, you will know that sex is sacred, holy. Then you live it, then you delight in it; and as naturally as it has come, it goes of its own accord. By the age of forty-two, or somewhere near there, your interest in sex as such starts disappearing as naturally as it had come into being.

But it doesn't happen that way. Instead, you will be surprised when I say forty-two. You know people who are seventy, eighty, and yet they have not gone beyond their obsession with sex. You know "dirty old men." They are victims of the society because they could not be natural. It is a hangover, because they repressed their sexuality when they should have enjoyed and delighted in it. In those moments of sexual delight they were not totally in it. They were not orgasmic, they were half-hearted.

Whenever you are half-hearted in anything, it lingers longer. If you are sitting at your table and eating, and if you eat only half-heartedly then your hunger will remain. Then you will continue to think about food the whole day. You can try fasting and you will see: you will continuously think about food! But if you have eaten well, and when I say that, I don't mean only that you have stuffed your stomach. Then it is not necessarily the case that you have eaten well. You might have stuffed yourself, but eating well is an art. It is not just stuffing yourself, it is a great art—to taste the food, to smell the food, to touch it, chew it, to digest the food, and to digest it as divine. It is divine; it is a gift.

Hindus say, *Anam Brahma*, food is divine, a gift from God. With deep respect you eat, and while eating you forget everything else, because eating is prayer. It is existential prayer. You are eating God, and God is going to give you nourishment. It is a gift to be accepted with deep love and gratitude.

And you don't stuff the body, because stuffing the body is being antagonistic to the body. It is the other pole. There are people who are obsessed with fasting, and there are people who are obsessed with stuffing themselves. Both are wrong, because in both ways the body loses balance. A real lover of the body eats only to the point where the body feels perfectly quiet, balanced, tranquil; where the body feels to be neither leaning to the left nor to the right, but just in the middle. It is an art to understand the language of the body, to understand the language of your stomach, to understand what is needed and to give only that which is needed, and to give that in an artistic way, in an aesthetic way.

Animals eat, man eats—what is the difference? Man makes a great, aesthetic experience out of eating. What is the point of having a beautiful dining table? What is the point of having candles burning there? What is the point of asking friends to come and participate? It is to make it an art, not just stuffing yourself. But these are outward signs of the art; the inward signs are to understand the language of your body and to listen to it, to be sensitive to its needs. Then you eat, and the whole day you will not think of food at all. Only when the body is hungry again will the remembrance come. Then it is natural.

With sex the same happens. If you have no "anti" attitude about it, then you take it as a natural, divine gift. With great gratitude you enjoy it; with prayerfulness you enjoy it.

Tantra says that before you make love to a woman or to a man, you should first pray because it is going to be a divine meeting of energies. A fragrance of godliness will surround you. Wherever two lovers are, there is godliness. Wherever two lovers' energies are meeting and mingling, there is life, alive, at its best—a divine energy surrounds you. Churches are empty, but love chambers are full of godliness. If you have tasted love the way Tantra says to taste it, if you have known love the way Tao says to know it, then by the time you reach forty-two, sex starts disappearing of its own accord. And you say good-bye to it with deep gratitude, because you are fulfilled. It has been delightful, it has been a blessing; you say good-bye to it.

And forty-two is the age for meditation, the right age. Sex disappears and that overflowing energy is no longer there. One becomes more tranquil. Passion has gone and now compassion arises. Now there is no more fever; one is not so interested in the "other." With sex disappearing, the other is no longer a focus. One starts returning to one's own source; the return journey starts.

Sex is transcended not by your effort. It happens if you have lived it totally. So my suggestion is, drop all condemnation, all antilife attitudes and accept the facts: sex is, so who are you to deny it? And who is trying to deny it, to go beyond it? It is just the ego.

Remember, sex creates the greatest problem for the ego. There are two types of people: very egoistic people are always against sex; humble people are never against it. But who listens to humble people? In fact, humble people don't go around preaching, only egoists.

Why is there a conflict between sex and ego? Because sex is something in your life where you cannot be egoistic, where the other becomes more important than you. Your woman, your man, becomes more important than you. In every other case, *you* remain the most important. In a love relationship the other becomes very, very important, tremendously important. You become a satellite and the other becomes the nucleus; and the same is happening for the other: you become the nucleus and he or she becomes a satellite. It is a reciprocal surrender. Both are surrendering to the god of love, and both become humble.

Sex is the only energy that gives you hints that there is something that you cannot control. Money you can control, politics you can control, the market you can control, knowledge you can control, science, morality, all these things you can control. Somewhere, sex brings in a totally different world; you cannot control it. And the ego is a great controller. It is happy if it can control; it is unhappy if it cannot control. So there is a conflict between the ego and sex.

Remember, it is a losing battle. The ego cannot win it because ego is just superficial. Sex is very deep-rooted. Sex is your life; ego is just your mind, your head. Sex has roots all over you; ego has roots only in your ideas—very superficial, just in the head.

So who is trying to go beyond biological, sexual attraction? The head is trying to control sex. If you are too much in the head then you want to go beyond your sexual feelings because sex brings you down to the guts. It does not allow you to remain hanging in the head. Everything else you can manage from there; sex you cannot manage from there. You cannot make love with your head. You have to come down, you have to descend from your heights, you have to come closer to earth.

Sex is humiliating to the ego, so egoistic people are always against sex. They go on finding ways and means to transcend it. They can never transcend it. They can, at the most, become perverted. Their whole effort from the very beginning is doomed to failure.

I have heard:

> *A boss was interviewing applicants to replace his private secretary who was resigning because of expectant motherhood. The boss's right-hand man sat with him as he looked the applicants over. The first girl was a beautiful, buxom blond. She turned out to be intelligent, and had excellent secretarial skills. The second was a dark-haired beauty who was even more intelligent and proficient than the first. The third one was cross-eyed, had buck teeth, weighed one hundred and ninety pounds, and had almost no skills. After interviewing all three candidates, the boss informed his associate that he was hiring the third applicant.*
>
> *"But why?" asked the astonished employee.*
>
> *"Well," boomed the boss, "in the first place, she looks very intelligent to me! In the second place, it is none of your damned business, and in the third place, she is my wife's sister."*

So you may pretend that you have won over sex, but an undercurrent remains. You may rationalize, you may find reasons, you may pretend, you may create a hard shell around you, but deep down the real reason, the reality, will stand untouched: "She is my wife's sister"—that is the real reason. "She looks intelligent"—that is just a rationalization. "And it is none of your damned business"—that is being annoyed and irritated because you are afraid that the other may find out the real case! But the real case will explode no matter what you do; you cannot hide it, it is not possible.

So you can try to control sex, but an undercurrent of sexuality will run through your being, and it will show itself in many ways. Out of all your rationalizations, it will again and again raise its head.

I will not suggest that you make any effort to go beyond your sexuality. What I suggest is just the contrary: forget about going beyond it. Move into it as deeply as you can. While the energy is there, move as deeply as you can, love as deeply as you can, and make an art of it. It is not just to be "done."

That is the whole meaning of Tantra, making an art of love-making. There are subtle nuances, which only people who enter with a great aesthetic sense will be able to know. Otherwise, you can make love for your whole life and still remain unsatisfied because you don't know that real satisfaction is something very aesthetic. It is like a subtle music arising in your soul. If through sex you fall into harmony, if through love you become non-tense and relaxed, if love is not just throwing out energy because you don't know what else to do with it, if it is not just a relief but a relaxation, if you relax into your partner and your partner relaxes into you, if for a few seconds, for a few moments or a few hours you forget who you are and you are completely lost in oblivion, you will come out of it purer, more innocent, more virgin. And you will have a different type of being: at ease, centered, rooted.

If this happens, one day suddenly you will see that the flood has gone and it has left you very, very rich. You will not be sorry that it has gone. You will be thankful, because now richer worlds open. When sex leaves you, the doors of meditation open. When sex leaves you, then you are not trying to lose yourself in the other. You become capable of losing yourself in yourself. Now another world of orgasm, inner orgasm, of being with oneself, arises.

But that arises only through being with the other. One grows, matures through the other. Then a moment comes when you can be alone, tremendously happy. There is no need for any other. The need has disappeared but you have learned much through it, you have learned much about yourself. The other became the mirror. And you have not broken the mirror! You have learned so much about yourself, now there is no need to look into the mirror. You can close your eyes and you can see your face there. But you would not be able to see that face if there had been no mirror from the very beginning.

Let your woman be your mirror; let your man be your mirror. Look into your partner's eyes and see your face; move into your partner to know yourself. Then one day the mirror will not be needed. But you will not be against the mirror! You will be so grateful to it, how can you be against it? You will be so thankful, how can you be against it? Then, transcendence happens.

Transcendence is not repression. Transcendence is a natural growth of your being; you grow above, you go beyond, just as a seed breaks and a sprout starts rising above the ground. When sex disappears, the seed disappears.

In sex, you were able to give birth to somebody else, a child. When sex disappears, the whole energy starts giving birth to yourself. This is what Hindus have called *dwija*, the twice-born. One birth has been given to you by your parents, the other birth is waiting. It has to be given to you by yourself. You have to father and mother yourself. Then your whole energy is turning in—it becomes an inner circle.

Right now it will be difficult for you to make an inner circle. It will be easier to connect it with another pole—a woman or a man—and then the circle becomes complete. Then you can enjoy the blessings of the circle. But by and by you *will* be able to make the inner circle, because inside you also you are man and woman, woman and man. Nobody is just man and nobody is just woman, because you come from the communion of a man and a woman. Both have participated; your mother has given something to you and you father has given something to you. Fifty-fifty, they have contributed to you. Both are there. There is a possibility that both can meet inside you. Again your father and mother can love inside you. Then your reality will be born. Once they met when your body was born; now, if they can meet inside you, your soul will be born.

That's what transcendence of sex is; it is a higher sex.

Let me tell you this: when you transcend sex, you reach to a higher sex. Ordinary sex is gross, higher sex is not gross at all. Ordinary sex is outward-moving, higher sex is inward-moving. In ordinary sex, two bodies meet, and the meeting happens on the outside. In higher sex, your own inner energies meet. It is not physical, it is spiritual, it is Tantra. Tantra is transcendence. If you don't understand this and you go on fighting with sex . . .

The question has been asked by a woman whom I know is passing through some critical moments in her mind. She would like to be independent, but it is too early. She would like not to be bothered by anybody else but it is too early, and it is too egoistic. Right now transcendence is not possible, only repression is possible. And if you repress now, in your old age you will repent because then things become messed up.

Each thing has its own right time. Each thing has to be done in its moment. While young, don't be afraid of love, and don't be afraid of sex. If you are afraid while you are young, in old age you will become obsessed; and then it will be difficult to move deeply into love, and the mind will remain obsessed.

It is my understanding that people, if they have lived rightly, lovingly, naturally, then by the forty-second year they start going beyond sex. If they have not lived naturally and they have been fighting with sex, then forty-two becomes their most dangerous time—because by the time they are forty-two their energies are declining. When you are young you can repress something because you are energetic. Look at the irony of it! A young person can repress his or her sexuality very easily because young people have the energy to repress it. They can just put it down and sit on it. When the energies are declining, then that repressed sexuality will assert itself and you will not be able to control it.

I have heard an anecdote:

> *A sixty-five-year-old man visited the office of his son, who was a doctor, and asked for something that would increase his sexual potential. The son gave his father a shot, and then refused to accept a fee. Nevertheless, the old man insisted on giving him ten dollars. A week later the old man was back for another injection, and this time handed his son twenty dollars.*
>
> *"But Pop, the shots are only ten dollars."*
>
> *"Take it!" said Stein. "The extra ten is from Momma."*

That will continue. So before that happens to you, please be finished with it. Don't wait for old age, because then things go ugly. Then everything goes out of season.

? I know my love stinks, so why do I cling to the smell?

We live according to the past. Our lives are rooted in the dead past, we are conditioned by the past. The past is very powerful, that's why you go on living in a certain pattern; even if it stinks, you will go on repeating it. You don't know what else to do, you have become conditioned to it. It is a mechanical phenomenon.

And this is not only so with you, it is so with almost every human being unless he or she becomes a buddha.

To become a buddha means to get rid of the past and to live in the present. The past is immense, huge, enormous. For millions of lives you have lived in a certain way. Now you may have become aware that your love stinks, but that awareness is also not very deep; it is very superficial. If it becomes really deep, if it penetrates to the very core of your being, you will immediately jump out of it.

If your house is on fire, you will not ask anybody how to get out of it. You will not consult the *Encyclopedia Britannica*, nor will you wait for some wise man to come and tell you. You will not consider whether it is appropriate to jump out of the window or not, you won't bother about any of that. Even if you are taking a bath, naked, you will jump naked out of the window! You won't even bother about clothes. When the house is on fire, your life is at risk; now everything else is secondary.

If your love stinks—if this has really become your experience—then you will come out of it. You will not simply ask a question, you will jump out of it.

But I think it is just an intellectual idea, because each time you are in love some misery arises. Each time there is some conflict, some struggle, some fight, some jealousy, some possessiveness. So you have started taking an intellectual standpoint: "My love stinks, so why do I cling to the smell?" Because it is not yet really an existential experience for you.

And it is your own smell! One becomes accustomed to one's own smell. That's why when people are alone they don't experience that smell, they experience it only when they are together with somebody else. When you are in love, then you start showing your real face. Love is a mirror. The other starts functioning as a mirror. Every relationship becomes a mirror. Alone, you don't experience your own smell, you cannot; one becomes immune to it. You have lived with it so long, how can you smell it? It is only with the other that you start feeling that *he* stinks and he starts feeling that *you* stink. And the fight starts. That is the story of all the couples all over the world.

> *"Where are you going with that goat, Juan?" asked the policeman.*
>
> *"I'm taking him home to keep as a pet!" replied Juan.*
>
> *"In the house?"*
>
> *"Sure thing."*
>
> *"But what about the smell?"*
>
> *"So what? He ain't gonna mind the smell!"*

Your own smell is not disturbing to you. In fact, if it suddenly disappears you will feel a little jolted, you will feel a little uprooted. You will not feel like your natural self; you will feel something has gone wrong. If you love and there is no jealousy, you will start wondering whether you love or not. What kind of love is this? There seems to be no jealousy!

Yes, your love stinks, as everybody else's love stinks, but you feel it only when you are in relationship. You have not yet felt that it really has something to do with you. Deep down you still feel it must be something wrong with the other. That's how the mind functions: it throws the responsibility on the other. It accepts itself and it is always finding faults in others.

> *Several people are sitting in the front row of a movie theater. The show has already begun when suddenly there is a terrible smell. One of the spectators turns to the man sitting beside him and asks, "Did you shit in your trousers?"*
>
> *The man beside him answers, "Yes, why?"*

People accept themselves totally! Whatever they are doing is right: "Why? What is wrong in it?" They are his trousers, so who are you to interfere? And freedom is everybody's birthright!

If your love stinks, then try to find out what exactly it is that stinks. It is not love, it is something else. Love itself has a fragrance; it can't stink, it is a lotus flower. Something else must be in it—jealousy, possessiveness. But you have not mentioned jealousy and possessiveness. You are hiding them. Love never stinks, it cannot; that is not the nature of love. Please try to see exactly what it is that creates the trouble. And I am not saying to repress it. All that is needed is a clarity about it, what it is.

If it is jealousy, then I would only suggest one thing: be more watchful of your jealousy. When it arises next time, rather than getting angry close your doors, sit silently, sit in meditation and watch your jealousy. See exactly what it is. It will surround you like smoke, dirty smoke. It will suffocate you. You would like to go out and do something, but don't do anything. Just be in a state of non-doing, because anything done in a moment of jealousy is going to be destructive. Just watch.

And I am not saying repress it, because that is again doing something. People are either expressive or repressive, and both ways are wrong. If you express you become destructive to the other person. Whoever is your victim suffers, and he is going to take revenge. He may not take revenge consciously, but unconsciously it is going to happen.

Just a few months ago, KB fell in love with a woman. Nothing extraordinary about it, but his girlfriend Deeksha got mad! She could not accept the idea. For centuries we have been told that if a man loves you or a woman loves you and the man or the woman goes to somebody else, that is a rejection of you.

That is utter nonsense. It is not rejection; in fact, it is just the opposite. If a man loves the woman and he enjoys the woman, he starts fantasizing how it will be with other women. It is really the joy that this woman has given him that triggers his fancy. It is not that he is rejecting this woman; it is really an indication that this woman has been such a nourishment that he would like to see and know how other women are. And if he is allowed, he is not likely to go very far, he will come back because with the other woman it may be novelty, it will be something new, but it can't be that nourishing because there will not be any intimacy. It will have something empty about it. It will be sex without love.

Love needs time to grow, it needs intimacy to grow. It needs a really long time. It is not a seasonal flower that is there within three or four weeks, but then within another few weeks it is gone. It is a long process of growing intimacy. Slowly, two persons melt and merge into each other; then it becomes nourishing. So the other woman, or the other man, cannot be nourishing. It may be just an adventure, a thrill. But then suddenly the feeling will arise—it is bound to arise—that it was good as fun, but not very nourishing. And the person will be back.

And KB would have been back, but Deeksha went mad. She behaved just like any other woman! But I was watching to see if sooner or later she was going to take revenge. And now she is taking revenge. KB fell ill, he was in the hospital, and Deeksha had a little freedom—she fell in love with her own handyman! He really proved handy! So now KB is in hell.

There is no need to be so worried about it. I have sent KB a message: "Wait, don't be worried. Just let her take revenge. It is good that her unconscious burden has a chance to be finished."

If we understand each other a little more, if we understand human nature a little more, there should be no jealousy. But it is a past heritage of centuries. It is not so easy to get rid of it, I am not saying you can just drop it right now. You will have to meditate over it. Whenever it possesses you, meditate over it. Slowly, the meditation will create the distance between you and the jealousy. And the greater the distance the less jealousy will arise. One day, when there is no jealousy, your love releases such a fragrance that no flower can compete with it. All flowers are poor compared to the flowering of love.

But your love is crippled because of jealousy and possessiveness and anger. It is not love that stinks, remember, because I have seen people who think it is love that stinks so they close up, they become closed, they stop loving. That's what has happened to millions of monks and nuns down the ages: they became closed to love, they dropped the whole idea of love. Rather than dropping jealousy, which would have been a revolution, rather than dropping possessiveness, which would have been something of immense value, they dropped love. That is easy, that is not much; anybody can do that.

To be a monk or a nun is very easy, but to love and not to be jealous, to love and not to be possessive, to love and let the other have all their freedom, is really a great achievement. Only then will you experience love and its fragrance.

LOVE AND THE ART OF NON-DOING

There are things which only happen, which cannot be done.

Doing is the way of very ordinary things, mundane things. You can do something to earn money, you can do something to be powerful, you can do something to have prestige; but you cannot do anything as far as love is concerned, gratitude is concerned, silence is concerned. It is significant to understand that "doing" means the world, and non-doing means that which is beyond the world—where things *happen*, where only the tide brings you to the shore. If you swim, you miss. If you *do* something, you will *un*do it; because all doing is mundane.

Very few people come to know the secret of non-doing and allowing things to happen. If you want great things—things that are beyond the small reach of human hands, human mind, human abilities—then you will have to learn the art of non-doing. I call it meditation.

It is a trouble, because the moment you give a name to it, immediately people start asking how to "do" it. And you cannot say that they are wrong, because the very word "meditation" creates the idea of doing. They have their doctorate, they have done a thousand and one things; when they hear the word "meditation" they ask, "So just tell us how to do it." And meditation basically means the beginning of non-doing, relaxing, going with the tide—just being a leaf in the breeze, or a cloud moving with the winds.

Never ask a cloud, "Where are you going?" He himself does not know; he has no address, he has no destiny. If the winds change he was going to the south, he starts moving towards the north. The cloud does not say to the winds, "This is absolutely illogical. We were moving south, now we are moving north. What is the point of it all?" No, he simply starts moving north as easily as he was moving south. To him, south, north, east, west, don't make any difference. Just to move with the wind, with no desire, with no goal, nowhere to reach; he is just enjoying the journey. Meditation makes you a cloud—of consciousness. Then there is no goal.

Never ask a meditator, "Why are you meditating?" because that question is irrelevant. Meditation is in itself the goal and the way together.

Lao Tzu is one of the most important figures in the history of non-doing. If history is to be written rightly then there should be two kinds of histories. The history of doers includes Genghis Khan, Tamerlane, Nadirshah, Alexander, Napoleon Bonaparte, Ivan the Terrible, Joseph Stalin, Adolf Hitler, Benito Mussolini; these are the people who belong to the world of doing. There should be another history, a higher history, a real history—of human consciousness, of human evolution. This is the history of Lao Tzu, Chuang Tzu, Lieh Tzu, Gautam Buddha, Mahavira, Bodhidharma; a totally different kind.

Lao Tzu became enlightened sitting under a tree. A leaf had just started falling: it was in the autumn and there was no hurry; the leaf was coming down zigzag with the wind, slowly. He watched the leaf. The leaf came down and settled on the ground, and as he watched the leaf falling and settling, something settled in him. From that moment, he became a non-doer. The winds come on their own, and existence takes care.

Lao Tzu's whole teaching was the watercourse way: just go with the water wherever it is going, don't swim. But the mind always wants to *do* something, because then the credit goes to the ego. If you just go with the tide, the credit goes to the tide, not to you. If you swim, there is a chance that you can have a greater ego: "I managed to cross the English Channel!"

But existence gives you birth, gives you life, gives you love; it gives you everything that is invaluable, everything you cannot purchase with money. Only those who are ready to give the whole credit of their lives to existence realize the beauty and the benediction of non-doing.

It is not a question of doing. It is a question of being absent as an ego, letting things happen.

Let go—just these two words contain the whole experience.

In life you are trying to do everything. Please, leave a few things for non-doing, because those are the only valuable things.

There are people who are trying to love, because from the very beginning the mother is saying to the child, "You have to love me because I am your mother." Now she is making love also a logical syllogism—"because I am your mother." She is not allowing love to grow on its own, it has to be forced.

The father is saying, "Love me, I am your father." And the

child is so helpless that all that he can do is pretend. What else can he do? He can smile, he can give a kiss, and he knows that it is all pretension: he does not mean it, it is all phony. It is not coming from him. But because you are his daddy, you are his mommy, you are this, you are that. They are spoiling one of the most precious experiences of life.

Then wives are telling husbands, "You have to love me, I am your wife." Strange. Husbands are saying, "You have to love me. I am your husband, it is my birthright." Love cannot be demanded. If it comes your way, be thankful; if it does not come, wait. Even in you're waiting, there should be no complaint, because you don't have any right. Love is nobody's right, no constitution can give you the right to experience love. But they are all destroying everything, then wives are smiling, husbands are hugging.

One of America's most famous authors, Dale Carnegie, writes that every husband should tell his wife at least three times a day, "I love you, darling." Are you insane? But he means it, and it works; and many people, millions of people, are practicing Dale Carnegie followers. "When you come home, bring ice cream, flowers, roses, to show that you love your wife," as if love needs to be shown, proved materially, pragmatically, linguistically, verbalized again and again so that nobody forgets it. If you don't tell your wife for a few days that "I love you" she will count how many days have passed, and she will become more and more suspicious that you must be saying it to somebody else, because her quota is being cut. Love is a quantity. "If he is not bringing ice cream anymore, that ice cream must be going somewhere else, and this cannot be tolerated."

We have created a society which believes only in "doings," while the spiritual part of our being remains starved because it needs something which is not done but *happens.* Not that you manage to say "I love you," but that suddenly you find yourself saying that you love. You yourself are surprised by what you are saying.

You have not rehearsed it in your mind first and then repeated it, no; it is spontaneous.

And in fact, the real moments of love remain unspoken. When you are really feeling love, that very feeling creates around you a certain radiance that says everything that you cannot say, that can never be said.

But instead we manage everything, we turn everything into a "doing" and the ultimate result is that slowly hypocrisy becomes our very characteristic. We forget completely that it is hypocrisy. And in the mind, in the being of a person who is a hypocrite, anything of the world of non-doing is impossible. You can go on doing more and more; you will become almost a robot.

So whenever you have suddenly an experience of *happening*, take it as a gift from existence and make that moment the herald of a new lifestyle. Just allow a few moments in twenty-four hours when you are not doing anything, just allowing existence to do something to you. And windows will start opening in you, windows that will connect you with the universal, the immortal.

? It feels to me that much of my own "doing" is to avoid boredom. Can you talk about the nature of the experiences we call boredom and restlessness?

Boredom and restlessness are deeply related. Whenever you feel boredom, then you feel restlessness. Restlessness is a by-product of boredom.

Try to understand the mechanism. Whenever you feel bored you want to move away from that situation. If somebody is saying something and you are getting bored, you start becoming fidgety. This is a subtle indication that you want to move away from this place, from this person, from this nonsense talk. Your body starts moving. Of course, out of politeness you suppress it, but the body is already on the move because the body is more authentic than the mind, the body is more honest and sincere than the mind. The mind is trying to be polite, smiling. You say, "How interesting!" but inside you are saying, "How boring! I have listened to this story so many times and you are telling it again!"

I have heard a story about Albert Einstein's wife. Friends of Albert Einstein would come to visit, and of course Einstein would always tell some anecdotes, some jokes, and they would laugh. But one friend became curious; he noticed that whenever he came, and Einstein started telling stories, Frau Einstein would immediately start knitting or doing something. So he asked her, "The moment your husband starts telling some story or some joke, why do you start knitting?"

She said, "If I don't do anything, it will be tremendously difficult for me to tolerate because I have heard those stories and jokes a thousand and one times. You come to visit sometimes, I am *always* here. Whenever anybody comes he tells the same jokes, the same stories. If I didn't do something with my hands, I would become so fidgety that it would be impolite. So I have to move my restlessness into some work. Then I can hide my fidgetiness behind the work."

Whenever you feel bored you will feel restless. Restlessness is an indication of the body; the body is saying, "Move away from here. Go anywhere, but don't be here." But the mind goes on smiling, and the eyes go on sparkling, and you go on saying that you are listening and you have never heard such an interesting story. The mind is civilized; the body is still wild. The mind is human; the body is still animal. The mind is false; the body is true. The mind knows the rules and regulations, how to behave and how not to behave. So even if you meet a bore you say, "I am so happy, so glad to see you!" And deep down, if you were allowed, you would kill this man! He tempts you to murder. So you become fidgety, you feel restless.

If you listen to the body and run away, the restlessness will disappear. Try it! If somebody is boring you, simply start jumping and running around. Watch what happens—your restlessness will disappear, because restlessness simply shows that the energy does not want to be here. The energy is already on the move; the energy has already left this place. Now you are following the energy, so the restlessness disappears.

The real thing is to understand boredom, not restlessness. Boredom is a very significant phenomenon. Only man feels bored, no other animal. You cannot make a buffalo bored, impossible. Only man gets bored because only man is conscious. Consciousness is the cause. The more sensitive you are, the more alert you are, the more conscious you are, the more you will feel bored, and in more situations. A mediocre mind does not feel bored so easily. He goes on; he accepts whatsoever is happening as okay. He is not so alert. The more alert you become, the more fresh, the more you will feel as if a given situation is just a repetition, as if some situation is just intolerable, as if some situation is just stale. The more sensitive you are the more easily you will become bored.

Boredom is an indication of sensitivity. Trees are not bored, animals are not bored, rocks are not bored because they are not sensitive enough. This has to be one of the basic understandings about your boredom: it happens because you are sensitive.

But buddhas also are not bored. You cannot bore a buddha. Animals are not bored and buddhas are not bored, so boredom exists as a middle phenomenon between the animal and the buddha. For boredom, a little more intelligence and sensitivity is needed than is given to the animals. And if you want to get beyond boredom then you have to become *totally* sensitive. Then again the boredom disappears. But in the middle, the boredom is there.

If you become animal-like, then too boredom disappears. So you will find that people who live a very animalistic life are less bored. Eating, drinking, marrying—they are not very bored, but they are also not very sensitive. They live at the minimum, with only as much consciousness as is needed for a day-to-day routine life.

You will find that intellectuals, people who think too much, are more bored because they think, and in their thinking they can see that something is just repetitious.

Your life is full of repetitions. Every morning you get up in almost the same way as you have been getting up all your life. You take your breakfast in almost the same way. Then you go to the office—the same office, the same people, the same work. Then you come home—the same wife, the same husband, the same partner. If you get bored it is natural. It is very difficult for you to see any newness here; everything seems to be old, dust-covered.

I have heard an anecdote.

> *Mary Jane, the very good friend of a wealthy broker, opened her door cheerfully one day, then quickly attempted to close it when she discovered the person on the threshold to be her lover's wife.*
>
> *The wife leaned against the door and said, "Oh, let me in, dear. I don't intend to make a scene, just to have a small friendly discussion."*
>
> *With considerable nervousness Mary Jane let her enter, then said cautiously, "What do you want?"*
>
> *"Nothing much," said the wife, looking about. "I just want the answer to one question. Tell me, dear, just between us, what do you see in that dumb jerk?"*

The same husband every day becomes a dumb jerk; the same wife every day, you almost forget how she looks. If you are told to close your eyes and to remember your wife's face, you will find it impossible to remember. Many other women will come into your mind, the whole neighborhood, but not your wife. The whole relationship has become a continuous repetition. You make love, you hug your wife, you kiss your wife, but these are all empty gestures now. The glory and the glamour has disappeared long before.

A marriage is almost finished by the time the honeymoon is over, then you go on pretending. But behind those pretensions a deep boredom accumulates. Watch people walking on the street and you will see them completely bored. Everybody is bored, bored to death. Look at their faces—there is no aura of delight. Look at their eyes—they are dust-covered, no glimmer of inner happiness. They move from the office to home, from home to the office, and by and by the whole life becomes a mechanical routine, a constant repetition. And one day they die. Almost always people die without ever having been alive.

Bertrand Russell is reported to have said, "When I think back, I cannot find more than a few moments in my life when I was really alive, aflame." Can you remember how many moments in your life you were really aflame? Rarely it happens. One dreams about those moments, one imagines those moments, one hopes for those moments, but they almost never happen. Even if they do happen, sooner or later they also become repetitive. When you fall in love with a woman or a man you feel a miracle has happened, but by and by the miracle disappears and everything settles into a routine.

Boredom is the consciousness of repetition. Because animals cannot remember the past, they cannot feel bored. They cannot remember the past, so they cannot feel the repetition. The buffalo goes on eating the same grass every day with the same delight. You cannot. How can you eat the same grass every day with the same delight? You get fed up.

Hence, people try to change. They move into a new house, they bring a new car home, they divorce the old husband, they find a new love affair. But again, that new thing is going to become repetitive sooner or later. Changing places, changing partners, changing houses, is not going to do anything.

And whenever a society becomes very bored, people start moving from one town to another, from one job to another, from one wife to another, but sooner or later they realize that this is all nonsense. The same thing is going to happen again and again with every woman, with every man, with every house, with every car.

What to do then? Become more conscious. It is not a question of changing situations. Transform your being, become more conscious. If you become more conscious you will be able to see that each moment is new. But for that, much energy, a tremendous energy of consciousness is needed.

The wife is not the same, remember. You are in an illusion. Go back home and look again at your wife—she is not the same. Nobody can be the same; just appearances deceive. The trees are not the same as they were yesterday. How can they be? They have grown. Many leaves have fallen, new leaves have come. Look at the tree on your street—how many new leaves have come? Every day the old are falling and the new are coming. But you are not that conscious.

Either have no consciousness, then you cannot feel the repetition, or, have so much consciousness that in each repetition you can see something new. These are the two ways to get out of boredom.

Changing outside things is not going to help. It is just like rearranging the furniture in your room again and again. Whatever you do, you can put it this way or that way, it is the same furniture. There are many people who continuously think about how to manage things, where to put things, how to arrange them, where not to put them, and they go on changing things according to their ideas. But it is the same room, it is the same furniture. How long will you be able to deceive yourself in this way? By and by everything settles, the newness disappears.

You don't have a quality of consciousness that can go on finding the new again and again. For a dull mind, everything is old; for a totally alive mind there is nothing old under the sun, cannot be.

Everything is in flux. Every person is in flux, is riverlike. Persons are not dead things, how can they be the same? Are *you* the same? Between the time you woke up this morning and went out, and the time you went back home, a lot has happened. Some thoughts have disappeared from your mind, other thoughts have entered. You may have attained a new insight. You cannot go back home the same as you had left. The river is continuously flowing; it looks the same, but it is not the same. Old Heraclitus has said that you cannot step twice into the same river, because the river is never the same.

One thing is that *you* are not the same, and another thing is that *everything* is changing. . . . but then one has to live at the peak of consciousness. Either live like a buddha or live like a buffalo, then you will not be bored. Now the choice is yours.

I have never seen anybody the same. I'm always surprised by the newness that you bring every day. You may not be aware of it.

Remain capable of being surprised.

Let me tell you one anecdote.

A man entered a bar, deep in private thoughts of his own. He turned to a woman just passing and said, "Pardon me, miss, do you happen to have the time?"

In a strident voice she responded, "How dare you make such a proposition to me!"

The man snapped to attention in surprise and was uncomfortably aware that every pair of eyes in the place had turned in their direction. He mumbled, "I just asked the time, miss."

In a voice even louder the woman shrieked, "I will call the police if you say another word!"

Grabbing his drink and embarrassed very nearly to death, the man hastened to the far end of the room and huddled at a table, holding his breath and wondering how soon he could sneak out the door.

No more than half a minute had passed when the woman joined him. In a quiet voice she said, "I'm terribly sorry, sir, to have embarrassed you, but I am a psychology student at the university and I am writing a thesis on the reaction of human beings to sudden, shocking statements."

The man stared at her for three seconds, then he leaned back and bellowed, "You will do all that for me, all night, for just two dollars?"

And it is said that the woman fell down unconscious.

Maybe we don't allow our consciousness to rise higher because then life would be a constant surprise. You might not be able to manage it. That's why you have settled for a dull mind, there is some investment in it. You are not dull for no reason, you are dull for a certain purpose; if you were really alive then everything would be surprising and shocking. If you remain dull then nothing surprises you, nothing is shocking. The more dull *you* are, the more life seems dull to you. If you become more aware, life will also become more alive, livelier, and there is going to be difficulty.

You always live with dead expectations. Every day you come home and you expect certain behavior from your wife. Now look how you create your own misery: you expect a certain fixed behavior from your partner and then you want your partner to be new? You are asking the impossible! If you really want your wife, your husband, your partner to remain continuously new to you, don't expect. Come home always ready to be surprised and shocked, then the other *will* be new.

But instead, we expect the other to fulfill certain expectations. And we ourselves never allow our total, fluxlike freshness to be known to the other. We go on hiding, we don't expose ourselves, because the other may not be able to understand it at all.

Both the husband and the wife expect the other to behave in a certain way, and, of course, each of them manages the roles. We are not living life, we are living roles. The husband comes home, he forces himself into a certain role. By the time he enters the house, he is no longer an alive person, he is just a husband.

A husband means a certain type of expected behavior. At home, the woman is a wife and the man is a husband. Now when these two persons meet there are really four persons: the husband and wife, who are not real persons but just personas, masks, false patterns, expected behavior, duties, and all that, and the real persons hiding behind the masks.

Those real persons feel bored.

But you have invested much in your persona, in your mask. If you really want a life that has no boredom in it, drop all masks, be true. Sometimes it will be difficult, I know, but it is worth it. Be true. If you feel like loving your wife, love her; otherwise say you don't feel like it. What is happening right now is that the husband goes on making love to the wife, thinking of some actress. In his imagination he is not making love to this woman, he is making love to some other woman. And the same is true about the wife. Then things become boring because they are no longer alive. The intensity, the sharpness, is lost.

It happened on a railway platform. Mr. Johnson had weighed himself on one of those old-fashioned penny machines that delivers a card with a fortune printed on it.

The formidable Mrs. Johnson plucked it from her husband's fingers and said, "Let me see that. Oh, it says you are firm and resolute, have a decisive personality, are a leader of men, and are attractive to women."

Then she turned over the card, studied it for a moment, and said, "And they have got the weight wrong as well."

And no woman can tolerate it if her husband is attracted to other women. There is the whole point, the whole crux. If he is not attracted to other women, how can she expect that he will be attracted to her? If he is attracted to other women, only then can he be attracted to her, because she is also a woman. The wife wants him to be attracted to her and not to anybody else. Now this is asking something absurd. It is as if you are saying, "You are allowed to breathe only in my presence and when you go near somebody else, you are not allowed to breathe. How dare you breathe anywhere else?" Just breathe when the wife is there, just breathe when the husband is there, and don't breathe anywhere else. Of course, if you do that you will be dead, and you will not be able to breathe in front of your partner either.

Love has to be a way of life. You are to be loving. Only then can you love your wife or your husband. But the wife says, "No, you should not look at anybody else with a loving eye." Of course you manage to control yourself, because if you don't it creates such nuisance, but by and by the glimmer in your eyes disappears. If you cannot look anywhere else with love, by and by you cannot look at your own wife with love. The capacity disappears. And the same has happened to her. The same has happened to the whole of humanity. Then life is a boredom; then everybody is just waiting for death; then there are people constantly thinking of committing suicide.

Marcel has said somewhere that the only metaphysical problem facing humanity is suicide. And it is so, because people are so bored. It is simply amazing more people don't commit suicide, how they go on living. Life doesn't seem to give anything, all meaning seems to be lost, but still people go on dragging somehow, hoping that some day some miracle will happen and everything will be put right.

It never happens. *You* have to put it right; nobody else is going to put it right for you. No Messiah is going to come, don't wait for one. You have to be a light unto yourself.

Live more authentically. Drop the masks; they are a weight on your heart. Drop all falsities. Be exposed. Of course it is going to be troublesome, but that trouble is worth it because only after that trouble will you grow and become mature. And then nothing is holding back life. Each moment life reveals its newness, it is a constant miracle happening all around you, only you are hiding behind dead habits.

Become a buddha if you don't want to be bored. Live each moment as fully alert as possible, because only in full alertness will you be able to drop the mask. You have completely forgotten what your original face is. Even when you stand before the mirror in your bathroom and you are alone, nobody is there. Even standing before the mirror you don't see your original face in the mirror. There, too, you go on deceiving yourself.

Existence is available for those who are available to existence. And then, I tell you, there is no boredom. Life is infinite delight.

?

Would you please talk more about what you mean by intimacy? Particularly, when is staying together through difficult times in a marriage or partnership positive and when is it negative?

Marriage is a way to avoid intimacy. It is a trick to create a formal relationship. Intimacy is informal. If marriage arises out of intimacy, it is beautiful but if you are hoping that intimacy will arise out of marriage, you are hoping in vain. Of course, I know that many people, millions of people, have settled for marriage rather than for intimacy—because intimacy is growth and it is painful.

Marriage is very secure. It is safe. There is no growth in it. One is simply stuck. Marriage is a sexual arrangement; intimacy is a search for love. Marriage is a sort of prostitution, a permanent sort. One has got married to a woman or to a man; it is a permanent prostitution. The arrangement is economical, not psychological, not of the heart.

So remember, if marriage arises out of intimacy then it is beautiful. That means that everybody should have lived together before they get married. The honeymoon should not happen after marriage, it should happen before marriage. One should have lived the dark nights, the beautiful days, the sad moments, the happy moments, together. One should have looked into each other's eyes deeply, into each other's being.

How to decide? If your intimacy is helping you to grow and to become mature then it is positive and good and healthy, wholesome. If it is destructive and it is not allowing you to become mature, rather, it is helping you to remain childish, immature, then it is unhealthy. Any relationship that keeps you childish is destructive. Get out of it. Any relationship that gives you challenges to grow, to go on an adventure, to go deeper and higher into life. I am not saying that a positive partnership or marriage will not have problems, it will have *more* problems than the negative. A positive relationship will have more problems because every day new challenges will be there. But each time a problem is solved you will have gone a little higher; each time a challenge is taken you will find something has become integrated in your being.

A negative relationship has no problems, or at the most, pseudo-problems, so-called problems—not real problems. Have you not watched it? Wives and husbands fight over trivia. They are not real problems, and even if you fight over them they don't give you anything, they don't help your growth Watch wives and husbands, watch yourself. You may be a husband, a wife—just watch. If you are fighting over trivia—small things which don't mean anything anyway—then you will remain immature and childish.

Real problems, authentic problems, which really have to be

faced, create great turmoil in your being; they bring a cyclone. One has to face them, and never avoid them. And the trivial questions are an escape from the real questions. A husband and wife will fight over very small things: which film to go to and which not to go to; what color car has to be purchased, what model, what make; to what restaurant they are going this evening. Such trivia! These things do not make any difference. You are making too much fuss about such problems and if you focus on them, your relationship is not going to help you, or give you any integrity, any center. I will call that relationship negative.

The positive relationship will face real problems. For example, if you are angry or sad, you will be sad in front of your wife, you will not smile a false smile. And you will say, "I am sad." This has to be faced. If, walking on the road with your wife, you see a beautiful woman pass by and a great desire and longing arises in your heart, you will tell your wife that this woman created a great desire, stirred your heart. You will not avoid her. You will not take your eyes away or pretend that you have not seen the woman at all. Whether you pretend or not, your wife has already noticed it! It is impossible for her not to know because immediately your energy, your presence, changes. These are real problems.

Just getting married to a woman doesn't mean that you are no longer interested in any other woman. In fact, the day you are not interested in any other women, you will not be interested in your wife either. Why? For what? What has your wife got that is special? If you are no longer interested in women you will not be interested in your wife either. You are in love with her because you are in love with women, still. Your wife is a woman. And sometimes you come across another woman who enchants you. You will say it and you will face the turmoil that will arise. It is not trivia, because it will create jealousy, it will create a struggle, it will disturb all peace and you will not be able to sleep at night. The wife will be throwing pillows at you!

To be true creates real problems. To be authentic creates real problems. And say whatsoever is the case. Never demur, never look sideways. Look straight and be true, and help your partner to be true.

Yes, there are problems in real intimacy, more problems than in a negative state. If you are really intimate with your partner, how can you avoid the fact that you become interested in another person? You have to say it. That's part of love, part of intimacy. You expose yourself totally and you don't hold anything back. Even if during the night you dream a dream about another person, in the morning you can relate it to your partner.

I have heard about a film director. During the night he started talking to his girlfriend in his sleep, and he was talking aloud. He was saying such beautiful things, and his wife woke up. She started staring at him, listening hard to what he was saying. When you are married, even in your dreams you remain afraid of your wife, so suddenly he woke up and became afraid. What was he saying? He felt his wife looking at him and with great presence of mind, without opening his eyes to give any indication that he was awake, he said, "Cut! Now to the next scene," as if he was directing a film!

If you really love the woman, in the morning you will tell her your dream, that you made love to another woman in the night in your dream. Everything has to be shared. The whole heart has to be shared.

Intimacy means that there is no privacy. You don't carry anything private now, at least with the person you are intimate with, you drop your privacy. You are nude and naked—good, bad, whatsoever you are, you open your heart. And whatever the cost you pay for it; whatever the trouble you go through with it. That brings growth.

And you help the other person also to drop all inhibitions,

screens, masks. In an intimate relationship one comes to see the original face of the other and one comes to show one's own original face. If a relationship helps you to find your original face then it is meditative, then it is spiritual. If your relationship simply helps you to create more and more masks and hypocrisies then it is irreligious.

Try to understand my definition. If my definition is understood then out of a hundred marriages, ninety-nine are irreligious because they are simply creating more and more falsity. From the very beginning the falsity starts.

I have heard:

> *The minister, casting an appraising eye over the bridal couple before him and the goodly crowd come to witness the ceremony, intoned, "If there is anyone here who knows why these two should not be joined together in wedlock, let him speak now or forever hold his peace."*
>
> *"I've got something to say," a voice rang out bold and clear.*
>
> *"You keep quiet!" snapped the minister. "You're the groom."*

From the very beginning! They are not even married yet. And that's how the life of a married couple starts. People keep quiet. They don't say anything. They don't say the truth at all. They pretend with lies. They smile when they don't want to smile, they kiss when they don't want to kiss. Naturally, when you kiss and you don't want to, the kiss is poisonous. Naturally, when you don't want to smile and you have to smile, your smile is ugly, it is political. And then somehow one gets accustomed to these things, one settles with the falsity, with the inauthenticity of life. And one consoles oneself in a thousand and one ways.

"Oh, we're very happy," insisted the husband. "Of course, once in a while my wife throws dishes at me. But that doesn't change the situation one bit, because if she hits me she's happy, and if she misses me I'm happy!"

One by and by comes to such an arrangement: both are happy.

The car in which the elderly couple were riding went over the cliff. It was an awful wreck.

"Where am I?" moaned the man when he opened his eyes. "In heaven?"

"No," said his dazed wife. "I'm still with you."

These settlements are hellish. What you know in the name of relationship is just a game of falseness and hypocrisy.

So remember it as a criterion: if you are growing more and becoming an individual, if life is happening more to you, if you are becoming more open, if more beauty is felt in existence, if more poetry is arising in your heart, if more love flows through you, more compassion, if you are becoming more aware, then the relationship is good. Carry on. Then it is not a marriage. Then it is intimacy.

But if the reverse is happening; if all poetry is disappearing and life is becoming prosaic; if all love is disappearing and life is becoming just a load, a dead load; if all song is dying and you are just living as a duty, then it is better to escape from this prison. It is better for you and it is better for the partner with whom you are living.

?

I feel really confused. You just keep on telling me, in one way or the other, that I am a complete crackpot to be with my boyfriend; but there is still something so strong in me that wants to stay in this relationship. If it

> **brings me closer to really and truly being myself to be alone and without relationship, I am definitely not getting it. If it means that this relationship is getting in the way, it hurts too much to even feel it. What is it that I am still not getting?**

The question is not what you are not getting, but that you are getting too many ideas of your own which have nothing to do with me. So let me tell you clearly and simply, that I'm not against any relationship; and particularly you and your boyfriend, who fit together so well! He's a nutcase, you are a crackpot—I will not disturb your relationship. Otherwise, the nutcase will disturb somebody else, the crackpot will disturb somebody else, and two more persons will be disturbed.

Just out of sheer compassion I want you to be together, to cling, whatever happens. What more can happen? He has become a nutcase; beyond that, the road comes to an end. You are a crackpot. Hang around each other, it is beautiful company! Yes, there is fighting, but there are moments of love too. You are so attached to him, and he's also attached to you. It always happens when nuts fall in love with each other, then no matter what hell they create for each other they remain together. That hell is their heaven.

I'm not against your relationship. What I'm saying is that your boyfriend should get out of being a nut and become a human being, and that you should get out of being a crackpot to be a human being—to relate as human beings, love as human beings. I'm the last person to disturb anybody's love. If I disturb it, I disturb it only to take you a little higher, to take your love to more juicy spaces.

You got it all wrong, but that is understandable. I was waiting for your question. I could have written the question myself, because I knew what would be going on in these two strange people's minds. And you yourself reported to me that since your boyfriend had gone to Goa, you enjoyed such peace and joy in those weeks.

When he informed you that he was coming back in a week, he had not yet come, but you started retraining yourself. You had to be ready to receive him, so you started becoming miserable. In those seven days while you were waiting for him to come back you again lost all joy, all peace. Now that he is here, you are again playing your old games, which are destructive to both of you.

I would not like to separate you, but I would like you to drop these ideas of being a crackpot, or being a nut. These are dangerous ideas, and if you carry a certain idea too long, it starts becoming a reality. You create your reality around yourself with your ideas—it is a projection.

Simply renounce your past and meet with each other as strangers. Say to your boyfriend, "Hello," and don't repeat inside your mind that, "This is that nutcase." Avoid that. Nutcases are not bad people, but after all they are nuts. You fit together very well, but the fit should be joyous. It should be a great blessing; you should help each other for your growth.

Fighting should stop. You are soft in your heart, and he is also very soft in his heart. I know many kinds of nuts and they are all soft inside. Just drop your coverings, your personalities, and don't clash with each other.

I am not against your relationship, but a relationship is not meant to be just for clashing with each other. Fighting is not love. Once in a while you are loving, but that is just so that you can go on fighting.

There is no need to fight at all. And whenever you are feeling too full of energy, you can do Dynamic Meditation. Why do you think I have created all these meditations for all kinds of nuts?—so they can enjoy one hour of being a nut, with a great idea that they are doing a spiritual meditation! It is simply to throw out their nuttiness without throwing it on anybody else, so that with others they can have a cooler, more peaceful, loving relationship.

I am not against any love, but if love creates hell, then I will not suggest that you go on living in misery. Then it is better for both of you—if you cannot create a beautiful space between you, then perhaps you are not born for each other. Give it a try, and beware of the fact that if you remain grumpy, your face continuously sad, then I am going to suggest that you part from each other.

You are simply a nut. He is a very qualified person, a *coconut*—he will understand me.

There is no need to lose hope. Give it a try, but this time make it a point that either your life becomes peaceful and joyous, or with peace and joy, you part from one another.

We are all strangers in the world. We meet suddenly, accidentally, on the road. It is good if we can help each other to be more authentic, more sincere, more loving; to be more meditative, to be more alert, to be more aware. Then our love relationship is a spiritual phenomenon. But if we are simply destroying each other, this is not even friendship; this is sheer enmity.

So you have to decide. You both sit together, outside in the open—not in your room, because there the fight starts. Sit outside where everybody is passing by, so you cannot fight. Have a nice conversation. Lovers forget completely how to have a nice conversation; they all start speaking Marathi. Have you heard Marathi? I cannot conceive that you can love anybody, talking in Marathi; it always sounds like you are fighting. Just at the opposite pole is another language in India, Bengali—you cannot fight in it. Even if you are fighting, it looks as if you are having a beautiful conversation.

Have a good, decisive conversation, and follow a very simple rule: that we are together to help each other, not to destroy each other; to create each other, not to kill each other. Then everything is perfectly okay. Nothing is wrong in you, separately, and nothing is wrong in Om, separately. But together you suddenly both become warriors.

When I say that your love should be a let-go, a non-doing, a freedom, I mean it should not be something forced. It should not be something dependent on law, on social conventions. I mean that the only binding force between two lovers is simply love, and nothing else. This love may go a long way or it may not go a long way. This love may last for your whole life, or it may be finished tomorrow. That's what I mean by let-go.

There are people who want licentiousness. That is not my meaning of let-go. I am not saying you should go on changing your partners every day. Again that will be forced. That would be moving from the one extreme of marriage, where you cannot change the partner, to the other extreme that you *have* to change your partner.

What I have said is, let it be a freedom. If you want to be together it is perfectly beautiful. The day you want to part, part lovingly, with gratefulness to each other for all those beautiful moments that you have given to each other.

The parting should be as beautiful as your meeting. It should even be *more* beautiful, because you have lived for so long together, you have grown roots into each other even though now you are deciding to leave one another. But the memories will haunt you. You have loved each other; it does not matter that now you feel it is difficult to be together, there was a time you wanted to be together for lifetimes. So part without any conflict, without any quarrel. You were two strangers who met, and again you are becoming strangers but with a great treasure that happened between the two of you. You have to be grateful to each other while parting.

But if the love continues, I have not said that you have to break it. I have said that you have not to do anything against it. If it goes on for your whole life, until you are in your grave, that too is good. And if it lasts only for one night and in the morning you feel that you are not for each other, but still you gave a beautiful night to each other, you have to be thankful for it.

Many people have misunderstood me. They think that I am telling people, "Change your partners as quickly and as often as possible." I am not saying that. I am simply saying that as long as love is the only binding force, be together. The moment you both start feeling that something has become past, that it is no longer present . . . you can drag on, but it will be deceiving each other. It is ugly to deceive a man you have loved; it is ugly to deceive a woman you have loved. It is better to be honest and say, "This is the time we should separate, because the love has gone and we are not capable of holding on to love."

There are things which come and go of their own accord. When you fell in love with someone, it was not you, *you* did not decide it. Suddenly it happened; you could not have given a reason for why it happened. You can simply say, "I found myself being in love." Just remember the first meeting, and also remember the way love comes; in the same way, it goes. One day, suddenly in the morning you wake up and you find that the love has left. The husband is there, you are there, but something between you that was a bridge, a constant flow of energy, has disappeared. You are two, but you are alone and the other is alone. That "together" is no longer there, and the mystery that was keeping it together is not in your hands. You cannot force it to come back.

Millions of couples are doing that, hoping that perhaps it will come back, hoping that praying may help, going to church may help, getting somebody's blessings may help, some marriage counselor may help—but nothing is going to help. Even if in some way you can catch hold of the same man again, you will find that he is not the same man, and he will find that you are not the same woman. It is better to become strangers again. What is wrong in it? Back when you were strangers, nothing was wrong. Back when you did not know the woman, did not know the man, everything was good. Now again that has happened and you are again strangers. It is nothing new! You should have been aware from the very beginning that something mysterious came in. You did not bring it in. Naturally, it can go any moment and you cannot hold it back.

All depends on love. If it remains a long time, good. If it remains only for a few moments, that too is good because *love* is good. The length of it is meaningless. It is possible to have, in just a few minutes, more intensity of love than you can have in a few years. And that intensity will give you something of the unknown, which so many years will simply dilute. So the length is irrelevant, the depth is the only thing to be thought about.

While you are in love, be totally immersed in it. And when it is gone, say good-bye and be totally finished with it. Don't let the idea linger in your mind. There are many strangers available in the world—who knows? Love has left you simply so that you can find a better stranger.

Life's ways are strange. Trust life. You may find somebody who proves to be a tremendous love, and then you will see that your first love was nothing compared to it.

And remember, some day this greater love can also disappear. But trust the life which has been giving you gifts again and again without your asking. Remain available.

The world is so full of beautiful people; there is no scarcity. And every individual has something unique which nobody else has. Every individual gives to his love a color, a poetry, a music that is his own, and that nobody else can give.

Trust life—that is my basic understanding, to trust life because we are born of life, we are children of life.

Trust life. Life has never betrayed anyone. Perhaps you have passed through one class and you have to enter into a second class, a higher grade, a more delicate love, a more sophisticated phenomenon—who knows? Just keep your heart open, and life never frustrates anybody.

PART III

From Relationship to Relating—Love as a State of Being

The capacity to be alone is the capacity to love. It may look paradoxical to you, but it is not. It is an existential truth: only those people who are capable of being alone are capable of love, of sharing, of going into the deepest core of the other person—without possessing the other, without becoming dependent on the other, without reducing the other to a thing, and without becoming addicted to the other. They allow the other absolute freedom, because they know that if the other leaves, they will be as happy as they are now. Their happiness cannot be taken by the other, because it is not give by the other.

Then why do they want to be together? It is no longer a need; it is a luxury. Try to understand it. Real persons love each other as a luxury; it is not a need. They enjoy sharing: they have so much joy, they would like to pour it into somebody. And they know how to play their life as a solo instrument.

The solo flute player knows how to enjoy his flute alone. And if he comes and finds a tabla player, a solo tabla player, they will enjoy being together and creating a harmony between the flute and the tabla. Both will enjoy it: they will both pour their richness into each other.

"LOVE" IS A VERB

Love is existential; fear is only the absence of love. And the problem with any absence is that you cannot do anything directly about it. Fear is like darkness. What can you do about darkness directly? You cannot drop it, you cannot throw it out, you cannot bring it in. There is no way to relate with darkness without bringing light in. The way to darkness goes via light. If you want darkness, put the light off; if you don't want darkness, put the light on. But you will have to do something with light, not with darkness at all.

The same is true about love and fear: love is light, fear is darkness. The person who becomes obsessed with fear will never be able to resolve the problem. It is like wrestling with darkness: you are bound to be exhausted sooner or later, tired and defeated. And the miracle is, defeated by something which is not there at all! And when one is defeated, one certainly feels how powerful the darkness is, how powerful the fear is, how powerful the ignorance is, how powerful the unconscious is. They are not powerful at all, they don't exist in the first place.

Never fight with the non-existential. That's where all the ancient religions got lost. Once you start fighting with the non-existential you are doomed. Your small river of consciousness will be lost in the non-existential desert, and it is infinite.

So don't make a problem out of fear. Love is the question. Something can be done about love immediately; there is no need to wait or postpone. Start loving! And it is a natural gift from existence to you, or from God, or from the whole, whichever term you like. If you are brought up in a religious way, then God; if you are not brought up in a religious way, then the whole, the universe, existence.

Remember, love is born with you; it is your intrinsic quality. All that is needed is to give it a way—to make a passage for it, to let it flow, to allow it to happen.

We are all blocking it, holding it back. We are so miserly about love, for the simple reason that we have been taught a certain economics. That economics is perfectly right about the outside world: if you have just so much money and you go on giving that money to people, soon you will be a beggar. By just giving away money you will lose it. This economics, this arithmetic has entered into our blood, bones, and marrow. It is true about the outside world, and nothing is wrong in it, but it is not true about the inner journey. There, a totally different arithmetic functions: the more you give, the more you have; the less you give, the less you have. If you don't give at all you will lose your natural qualities. They will become stagnant, closed; they will go underground. Finding no means of expression they will shrink and die.

It is like a musician: if he goes on playing on his guitar or on his flute, more and more music will come. It is not that by playing on the flute he is losing music—he is gaining. It is like a dancer: the more you dance, the more skillful you become. It is like painting: the more you paint, the better the paintings you create.

Once, while Picasso was painting, a critic and friend stopped him in the middle and said, "One question has been bothering me and I cannot wait anymore, I cannot contain it. I want to know: you have painted hundreds of paintings; which is your best painting?"

Picasso said, "This one that I am painting right now."

The critic said, "This one? What about the others that you have painted before?"

Picasso said, "They are all contained in it. And the next one that I do will be even better than this, because the more you paint, the greater is your skill, the greater is your art."

Such is love, such is joy—share it! In the beginning it will come only like dewdrops, because your miserliness has been in existence for so long, it is very ancient. But once even dewdrops of love have been shared, you will soon become capable of sharing the whole oceanic flood of your being, and you contain infinities.

Once you have known the higher mathematics of giving and gaining, you will find that just by giving you gain. Not that something is returned; in the very giving you are becoming richer. Then love starts spreading, radiating. And one day you will be surprised. Where is the fear? Even if you want to find it, you will not be able to find it at all.

Love is not a relationship. Love relates, but it is not a relationship. A relationship is something finished. A relationship is a noun; the full stop has come, the honeymoon is over. Now there is no joy, no enthusiasm, now all is finished. You can carry it on, just to keep your promises. You can carry it on because it is comfortable, convenient, cozy. You can carry it on because there is nothing else to do. You can carry it on because if you disrupt it, it is going to create much trouble for you.

Relationship means something complete, finished, closed. Love is never a relationship; love is relating. It is always a river, flowing, unending. Love knows no full stop; the honeymoon begins but never ends. It is not like a novel that starts at a certain point and ends at a certain point. It is an ongoing phenomenon. Lovers end, love continues. It is a continuum. It is a verb, not a noun.

Why do we reduce the beauty of relating to relationship? Why are we in such a hurry? Because to relate is insecure, and relationship is a security, relationship has a certainty. Relating is just a meeting of two strangers, maybe just an overnight stay and in the morning we say good-bye. Who knows what is going to happen tomorrow? And we are so afraid that we want to make it certain, we want to make it predictable. We would like tomorrow to be according to our ideas; we don't allow it freedom to have its own say. So we immediately reduce every verb to a noun.

You are in love with a woman or a man and immediately you start thinking of getting married. Make it a legal contract. Why? How does the law come into love? The law comes into love because love is not there. It is only a fantasy, and you know the fantasy will disappear. Before it disappears, settle down. Before it disappears, do something so it becomes impossible to separate.

In a better world, with more meditative people, with a little more enlightenment spread over the earth, people will love, love immensely, but their love will remain a relating, not a relationship. And I am not saying that their love will be only momentary. There is every possibility their love may go deeper than your love, may have a higher quality of intimacy, may have something more of poetry and more of godliness in it. There is every possibility that their love may last longer than your so-called relationships ever last. But it will not be guaranteed by the law, by the court, by the policeman. The guarantee will be inner. It will be a commitment from the heart, it will be a silent communion.

If you enjoy being with somebody, you would like to enjoy it more and more. If you enjoy the intimacy, you would like to explore the intimacy more and more. And there are a few flowers of love that bloom only after long intimacies. There are seasonal flowers too; within six weeks they are there in the sun, but within six weeks again they are gone forever. There are flowers which take years to bloom, and there are flowers that keep blooming for many years to come. The longer it takes, the deeper it goes.

But it has to be a commitment from one heart to another heart. It has not even to be verbalized, because to verbalize it is to profane it. It has to be a silent commitment: eye to eye, heart to heart, being to being. It has to be understood, not said.

It is so ugly seeing people going to the church or the court to get married. It is so ugly, so inhuman. It simply shows they can't trust themselves, they trust the authorities more than they trust their own inner voice. It shows that because they can't trust their love, they trust the law.

Forget relationships and learn how to relate. Once you are in a relationship you start taking each other for granted. That's what destroys all love affairs. The woman thinks she knows the man, the man thinks he knows the woman. Nobody knows! It is impossible to know the other, the other remains a mystery. And to take the other for granted is insulting, disrespectful.

To think that you know your partner is very ungrateful. How can you know the woman? How can you know the man? They are processes, they are not things. The woman that you knew yesterday is not there today. So much water has gone down the Ganges;

she is somebody else, totally different. Relate again, start again, don't take it for granted.

And the man who you slept with last night, look at his face again in the morning. He is no longer the same person, so much has changed. So much, incalculably much, has changed! That is the difference between a thing and a person. The furniture in the room is the same, but the man and the woman, they are no longer the same. Explore again, start again. That's what I mean by relating.

Relating means you are always starting, you are always trying to become acquainted. Again and again, you are introducing yourself to each other. You are trying to see the many facets of the other's personality. You are trying to penetrate deeper and deeper into his realm of inner feelings, into the deep recesses of her being. You are trying to unravel a mystery which cannot be unraveled.

That is the joy of love: the exploration of consciousness.

And if you relate, and don't reduce it to a relationship, then the other will become a mirror to you. Exploring the other, unawares you will be exploring yourself too. Getting deeper into the other, knowing his feelings, his thoughts, his deeper stirrings, you will be knowing your own deeper stirrings too. Lovers become mirrors to each other, and then love becomes a meditation.

Relationship is ugly, relating is beautiful.

In relationship both persons become blind to each other. Just think, how long has it been since you saw your lover eye to eye? How long has it been since you looked at your partner? Maybe years! Who looks at one's own wife? You have already taken it for granted that you know her. What more is there to look at? You are more interested in strangers than in the people you know; you know the whole topography of their bodies, you know how they respond, you know everything that has happened is going to happen again and again. It is a repetitive circle.

It is not so, it is not really so. Nothing ever repeats; everything is new every day. Just your eyes become old, your assumptions become old, your mirror gathers dust and you become incapable of reflecting the other.

Hence I say relate. By saying relate, I mean remain continuously on a honeymoon. Go on searching and seeking each other, finding new ways of loving each other, finding new ways of being with each other. And each person is such an infinite mystery, inexhaustible, unfathomable, that it is not possible that you can ever say, "I have known her," or, "I have known him." At the most you can say, "I have tried my best, but the mystery remains a mystery."

In fact the more you know, the more mysterious the other becomes. Then love is a constant adventure.

COUPLES COUNSELING

Insights for Living and Growing in Love

Editor's note: The following selections are taken from the evening meetings where Osho spoke directly with one or both partners in a couple, or with individuals who had come to ask him for insight into their problems in relationships.

When Telepathy Doesn't Work

It almost always happens that couples don't make things clear to each other. You hope that the other will understand, and the same is the case with the other: he or she thinks you will understand. Nobody understands! There is no communication, the problems have never been put forward clearly. You have to put things clearly: "I am not interfering with you, you can be who you are—I love you and I will go on loving you—but what about me?" Then some way can be found to work out the difficulties. You can remain together and still you can have your individuality and your freedom. If both partners really love each other, then they will be able to deal with the problem. But what really happens is that we never make things clear to each other. We go on hoping that the other will know telepathically. Nobody knows telepathically! The other is not a clairvoyant, you have to put it exactly: "two plus two is four"—like that. But what happens is that the real problem is not talked about.

Understanding the Need for Space

Create understanding, talk to each other, and understand that sometimes the other needs his space. And this is a problem: it may not happen at the same time for both of you. Sometimes you want to be with your partner, and he wants to be alone—nothing can be done about it. Then you have to understand and leave him alone. Sometimes you want to be alone but he wants to come to you—then tell him that you are helpless, but you need your space!

Just create more and more understanding. That's what lovers miss: love they have enough, but understanding none, not at all. That's why on the rocks of misunderstanding their love dies. Love cannot live alone without understanding. Alone, love is very foolish; with understanding, love can live a long life, a great life—of many joys shared, of many beautiful moments shared, of great poetic experiences. But that happens only through understanding.

Love can give you a small honeymoon, but that's all. Only understanding can give you deep intimacy. Then, even some day if you separate, the understanding will be with both of you, and that will be a gift of your love to each other. Lovers can separate, but the understanding that has been gained through the other, in the company of the other, will always be with you. That will remain as a gift, there can be no other gift. If you love a person, the only valuable gift that you can give to him is some quantity of understanding.

Dealing with Negative Feelings

Love is always beautiful in the beginning because you don't bring your destructive energies into it. In the beginning you bring your positive energies into it; both pool their energies positively, the thing goes simply fantastically. But then by and by the negative energies will start overflowing; you cannot hold them back forever. And once you have finished with your positive energy, the honeymoon is over and then comes the negative part. Then hell opens its doors and one cannot understand what has happened. Such a beautiful relationship, why is it on the rocks?

If one is alert from the very beginning, it can be saved. Pour your positive energies into it, but remember that sooner or later the negative will start coming up. And when the negative starts coming in, you have to release the negative energy alone. Go into a room by yourself and release the negative; there is no need to throw it on the other person.

If you want to scream and shout and be angry, go into a room and shut the door—shout, be angry, beat the pillow. Because nobody should be so violent as to throw things on other people. They have not done anything wrong to you, so why should you throw things on them? It is better to throw all that is negative into the dustbin. If you remain alert, you will be surprised to see that it can be done; and once the negative is released, again the positive is overflowing.

The negative can be released together only much later on in a relationship, when the relationship has become very well established. And then too it should be done only as a therapeutic measure. When the two partners of a relationship have become very alert, very positive, have become consolidated as one being and are able now to tolerate—and not only tolerate but use the other's negativity—they have to come to an agreement that now they will be negative together also, as a therapeutic measure.

Then too my suggestion is to let it be very conscious, not unconscious; let it be very deliberate. Make it a point that every night for one hour you will be negative with each other—let it be a game—rather than being negative anywhere, any time. Because people are not so alert—for twenty-four hours they are not alert—but for one hour you can both sit together and be negative. Then it will be a game, it will be like group therapy! After one hour you are finished with it and you don't carry the hangover, you don't bring it into your relationship.

The first step: the negative should be released alone. The second step: the negative should be released at a particular time with the agreement that you are both going to release the negative. Only at a third stage can one really become natural, and then there is no need to be afraid to harm the relationship or hurt the other. Then you can be both negative and positive, and both are beautiful, but only at the third stage.

At some point in the first stage you will start feeling that now your anger comes up no longer. You sit before the pillow, and the anger does not come. It will come for months, but one day you will find that it is no longer flowing, it has become meaningless, you cannot be angry alone. Then the first stage is over. But wait for the other person also to feel whether the first stage is over or not. If your partner's first stage is also complete, then the second stage starts. Then for one or two hours—whether morning or evening, you can decide—you set a time to express your negative feelings, deliberately. Take it as a psychodrama, it is impersonal. You don't hit hard—you hit, but still you don't hit the person. In fact you are simply throwing out your negativity. You are not accusing the other, you are not saying "You are bad"; you are simply saying "I am feeling that you are bad." You are not saying "You insulted me"; you say "I feel insulted." That is totally different, it is a deliberate game; "I am feeling insulted, so I will throw out my anger. You are closest to me so please function as an excuse for me" and the same is done by the other.

A moment will come when again you will find that this deliberate negativity does not function anymore. You sit for one hour together and nothing comes to you, nothing comes to your partner. Then that second stage is over.

Now the third stage, and the third stage is the whole of life. Now you are ready to be negative and positive as those feelings arise; you can be spontaneous.

This is how love becomes relating, becomes a quality of loving, becomes the natural state of your being.

Breaking Out of Old Relationship Patterns

Take twenty-four hours and write down everything that you can remember of how you have been sabotaging your relationships in the past, everything in detail. Look at it from every angle, and then don't repeat it. It will become a meditation, and whether love remains in a new relationship or not is immaterial. If you can remain aware in it, that will be worth something.

You know well, everybody knows because it is impossible not to know what you do in your relationships. In your saner moments you know well. In your insane moments you forget; that I know. So before these insane moments come, look. Write down all the things you always have done to sabotage your relationships, and keep a copy with you. Whenever something comes up where that old pattern might be repeated, look at it.

One should become alert by and by, and then everything is beautiful. Love is tremendously beautiful but it can become a hell. So first you pinpoint all these things, and then don't do them. And you will feel so happy, just in being able not to do them, you will feel a certain liberation. Those things are obsessive; they are like a neurosis, a sort of madness.

And whenever two people are in love they are there to be happy: nobody is there to be unhappy. But this is how everybody goes on being stupid. Sooner or later they start making each other unhappy, and then the whole point is lost. All dreams are shattered and again and again it becomes a wound.

The Feeling of "Something Missing"

Every lover feels that something is missing, because love is unfinished. It is a process, not a thing. Every lover is bound to feel that something is missing, but don't interpret it wrongly. It simply shows that love in itself is a dynamic thing. It is just like a river, always moving, always moving. In the very movement is the life of the river. Once it stops it becomes a stagnant thing; then it is no longer a river. The very word "river" implies a process, the very sound of it gives you the feeling of movement.

Love is a river; it is not a thing, a commodity. So don't think that something is missing; it is part of love's process. And it is good that it is not completed. When something is missing you have to do something, to move. That feeling of "something missing" is a call from higher and higher peaks. Not that when you reach them you will feel fulfilled. Love never feels fulfilled. It knows no fulfillment, but it is beautiful because then it is alive forever and ever.

In and Out of Tune

And you will always feel that something is not in tune. That too is natural, because when two persons are meeting, two different worlds are meeting. To expect that they will fit perfectly is to expect too much, is to expect the impossible, and that will create frustration. Something will always be out of tune. If you fit completely and there is nothing out of tune, the relationship will become stagnant. At the most there are a few moments when everything is in tune, rare moments. Even when they come you may not be able to catch them they are so swift, so rare. They have barely come and they are already gone, just a glimpse. And that glimpse can make you more frustrated, because then you will see more and more that things are out of tune.

This is how it has to be. Make all efforts to create that in-tuneness, but always be ready if it doesn't happen perfectly. And don't be worried about it, otherwise you will fall more and more out of tune. The feeling of being in tune comes only when you are not worried about it. It happens only when you are not tense about it, when you are not even expecting it—just out of the blue. It is a grace, a gift of existence, a gift of love.

Love is not a thing you can do. But by doing other things, love will happen. There are small things you can do—sitting together, looking at the moon, listening to music—nothing directly to do with love.

Love is very delicate, fragile. If you look at it, gaze at it directly, it will disappear. It comes only when you are unaware, doing something else. You cannot go directly, arrowlike. Love is not a target. It is a very subtle phenomenon. It is very shy. If you go direct, it will hide. If you do something direct, you will miss.

Cooling Passions

If love goes deeper, husbands and wives eventually become brothers and sisters. If love goes deeper, the sun energy becomes moon energy. The heat is gone, it is very cool. And when love goes deeper, a misunderstanding can also happen, because we have become accustomed to that fever, passion, that excitement, and now it looks all foolish. It is foolish! Now if you make love it looks silly; if you don't make love you feel as if something is missing because of the old habit.

So you will have to understand this coolness that is coming. And of course when you start feeling as one, a fear arises. A fear about what is happening because if the two of you become too much one person you will start forgetting the other. The other can be remembered only as "the other." Psychologists say that when a child starts learning and the word he first utters is "daddy" it hurts the mother, because she has been taking care of the child and she carried the child for nine months. She is with the child for twenty-four hours, but when the child utters his first word he says "daddy"? The father is just on the periphery and the mother is so close. She feels the child is betraying her!

But there is a reason to it: the mother is so one with the child that he cannot name her yet—that's the reason. She is so one with the child that he does not have the feeling that she is the "other." Daddy is not with the child so much; he comes and goes, in the morning he goes to the office and then he comes back in the evening and sometimes comes and plays with the child, and then he is gone again. He is always on the go, so he can be thought of as the "other." The mother is always there, so cannot yet think of her as separate. So first he names "daddy" and then, by and by, one day he learns the word "mommy." The third thing is that he will learn his own name because that is the most difficult thing for the child.

Now he can understand that the mother is also separate.

Sometimes he is hungry and she does not come, and sometimes he is wet and she is talking to somebody and doesn't notice it. He starts feeling that she is "other," not absolutely one with him. But he is one with himself, so the last thing he learns is his own name.

So when two lovers start becoming one, the fear arises: "Are you losing the other?" In a way you are, because the other will not be felt as the other, hence the idea of brotherly and sisterly love. Why? The brotherly and sisterly love has no excitement; it is a cool thing. It is very cool and calm—no passion, no sensuality, no sexuality.

And another thing is that the brother and sister have not chosen each other; it is a given phenomenon. One day you suddenly find that you are a sister to somebody or a brother to somebody; you have not chosen. Lovers you choose. In choosing a lover there is some ego involved. With a sister, with a brother, there is no ego involved. You have not chosen; it is a gift from existence. You cannot change, you cannot go to a judge and say that you want to divorce your sister and you don't want to be a brother to her anymore. Even if you decide not to be a brother, you still remain a brother. It doesn't make any difference what you want, there is no way to change it. It is irrevocable, you cannot revoke it.

When a husband and wife start feeling so much oneness, a fear arises: Have you started taking the other for granted? Has he become a brother or a sister, and so is no longer your choice, no longer involved with your ego, no longer a fulfillment of your ego's desires? All these fears arise. And in the past you had so much passion for one another, so much heat. You know now that it is foolish, but still, the past habit. . . . Sometimes one starts feeling that one is missing something, one feels a sort of emptiness. But don't look at it through the past. Look at it from the future.

Much is going to happen in this emptiness, much is going to happen in this intimacy—you will both disappear. It will become absolutely non-sexual, all heat will be gone, and then you will know a totally different quality of love. That quality that will arise in you that I call prayerfulness, meditativeness, pure awareness. But that is still in the future, that has not yet happened. You are on the way towards it. The past is gone and the future has not yet come.

This interim period will be a little hard, but don't think of the past. It is gone and it is gone forever; even if you try you cannot bring it back. It will be so foolish, it will feel so silly. You can drag it back, you can try, but you will fail and that will create more frustration. So don't even try. Just be loving in a new way. Let this new-moon love happen.

Hold each other, be loving to each other, care, and don't hanker for the heat because that heat was a kind of madness, it was a frenzy; it is good that it is gone. So you should think yourselves fortunate. Don't misunderstand it.

That is going to happen to each lover if you really listen to me and go deep. This is the depth you are asking for when you say that you want your love to go deep—this is the depth! The passionate love is a periphery, the compassionate love is at the center. That is the depth.

Just enjoy it: feel blissful, meditate together, dance together. If sex disappears, let it; don't force it to remain. If sometimes it happens, let it happen; if it disappears, let it disappear.

When the Thrill Is Gone

It is very difficult to be in love for a long time. It needs a great transformation in your being. Only then can you be in love for a long time. The ordinary love is a very momentary thing; it comes and goes, it starts and it ends, it has a beginning and it has an end. So, rather than rationalizing it, just look into the phenomenon that you are no longer in love. It will be hard! It is not that the love is still there but the energy is somehow no longer flowing. How can that happen? Love is the energy; if love is there, the energy will flow.

Maybe you are in love with your past love, that's possible. Maybe you are in love with your past memories—how beautiful things were and how the energy was flowing between you, and now it is not flowing. It is a hangover from the past. You are continuously thinking about the past, and you want the present also to be like the past. But it cannot be done. The present is totally different from the past, and it is good that it is different! If it were just a repetition of the past you would be fed up, completely bored.

So both partners have to look into the reality and try to find out the truth. If you are not in love anymore, then one thing can be done: you can be friends. There is no need to force yourselves to be lovers, and love cannot be forced. If you force it, it will be a hypocrisy and it will never satisfy anybody.

So just look into the thing. You have been lovers in the past, so at least you can be friends. Just look into it! Maybe if you decide to be friends, love may start flowing again, because again you will start being free, again you will start becoming individuals, again the security will be gone, again those elements that have destroyed your love will disappear. There is a possibility your love may start flowing again.

Just as you came together one day, now part and just be friends. First your love happened: you were friends, and then you just came together. Love arises out of friendship, and then sooner or later it becomes a relationship but without the friendship, then it dies. If you really want to revive it again—and I am not saying that it is a certainty, nobody can say anything about that, but—there is a possibility that it may revive. Or even if it doesn't revive, you can revive your loving energies with somebody else, your partner can love somebody else.

Always remember one thing: to be in love is good—that is

great virtue. If it is not flowing with one person, then it is better to let it be flowing with somebody else. But don't get stuck, otherwise you will suffer, you will make your partner suffer, you both will suffer. And the problem is that if you suffer long enough, you will become addicted to your suffering. Then you will start feeling a sort of enjoyment in the suffering itself. You may become masochists, and then it will be very difficult to get out of it. Right now the problem is so great.

Time to Say Good-bye

Talk to your partner, be truthful, and ask your partner also to be truthful. You have loved each other; at least this much you owe to each other, to be truthful, to be absolutely truthful. Put all the cards out on the table and don't try to hide; because that is not going to help. Only truth helps. Lies never help, they can only postpone the problem, and meanwhile the problem will be getting more and more roots in you. So the sooner the better.

Talk to your partner: be honest, even if it hurts. Tell your partner that it will hurt, but nothing to be worried about. You have been happy together; if it hurts, that too has to be faced. Be absolutely true—no finding of scapegoats, no witch hunting, no rationalization. Just be true. Look into yourself, show your heart, and help the partner also to be true. If love is finished, then be friends, there is no need to force it.

Never betray love. Lovers change. That is not a problem, that should not be a problem; we should not become attached too much to persons. Let there be only one commitment, and that has to be to love itself! Be in love with love, and everything else is secondary.

And be courageous, that courage will help. Otherwise you can both pretend that really you should stay together because of this and because of that, and you will go on being miserable. Never remain in misery for a single moment. Live dangerously because that is the only way to live.

The Agony and Ecstasy of Honesty

It is said that if every person starts saying the truth, then there will be no friendship in the world, no friendship at all: no lovers, no friendship, no marriage, nothing. All these things will simply disappear. Then it will be an encounter group, the whole situation will be an encounter group everywhere, in every situation.

But one can work slowly, particularly in intimate relationships. And if both are willing to go into the depth of sincerity and honesty, it pays. Your love will become deeper; it will have something of the beyond in it. If you can be honest and yet be together, if you can suffer the agony that honesty brings, then one day the ecstasy that honesty and only honesty can bring also follows.

Fear Is Not Always Wrong

Sometimes your energy needs to be left alone, something is happening within you that needs you to keep to yourself. And when you think of getting involved with somebody there is a hesitation that can feel like fear. But fear is not always wrong, remember. Nothing is always wrong; it depends. People have such ideas that fear is always wrong—it is not. Yes, sometimes it is wrong, sometimes it is not. Nothing is always right, and nothing is always wrong; everything depends on the context.

Right now your fear is perfectly right. It simply says to you "Don't get involved." It is not the fear of the new, not at all; that is a misinterpretation. It is simply fear that if you get entangled in somebody else's energy, you will lose the centering which is growing within you. You are becoming more centered, you are settling more in your being. You are coming to terms with your aloneness, and if you fall into a relationship, that will be dragging yourself out. When your movement is inwards, a relationship will take you out and that can create a contradiction. Hence the fear. The fear is really helpful in this case; it is showing you not to be foolish.

Remain alone. When the fear disappears, move into relationship; then it will be perfectly right. It will disappear—when its time is gone, when you have settled, when the energy is exactly as it should be inside you, then you can afford to go out. First one has to settle inside, then it is easy to go outside and it is not a distraction. In fact it becomes an enhancement of the inner because of the contrast. It becomes a little holiday from the inner, but you always come back. Then it is not destructive, it is creative. Then love helps meditation.

So simply wait. Listen to your fear and don't repress it. It will disappear on its own. When the energy is ready to go out, you will suddenly see one day that you are moving with somebody and there is no fear at all, your whole being is with you. When that happens, then move into relationship. Till then, avoid it.

Haunted

There is no need to forget! Go on remembering! You are trying to forget your lost lover—who can forget by trying? The more you try to forget, the more you remember, because even to forget you have to remember! Don't try to forget. Make it a meditation. Whenever you remember your old partner just close your eyes and remember the person as deeply as you can, and soon you will forget.

Imperfect Fit

Only two dead things can fit with each other totally. Life asserts itself, struggles, fights, clamors to be taken note of, tries to dominate. Life is a will to power, hence there is conflict. It is intrinsic to life itself. And nobody wants to be dominated; everybody wants to dominate. Relationship exists between these two.

A relationship is a miracle. It should not happen really, scientifically it should not happen. It happens because we are not yet scientific. And it is good that we are not yet scientific; and we are never going to be absolutely scientific. Something illogical will always remain in the heart of man. That keeps the flame of humanity alive; otherwise man becomes a machine. Only machines are utterly adjusted; a machine is never maladjusted.

So this is the problem facing every couple: when there is total conflict, all is destroyed. There is no bridge between you and the other; a relationship doesn't exist. If there is total adjustment, again the relationship disappears because there is no more flow, there is no more hope. Just between the two, exactly in the middle between adjustment and conflict, a little bit of adjustment, a little bit of conflict—and they go together. They look contradictory but they are complementary.

If one can remember that, one remains sane; otherwise a relationship can drive you insane. There are moments when it drives people insane, when it is too much to bear. So never ask for absolute adjustment. Just a little bit is more than enough. Feel grateful for that, and let the relationship remain a flow. Be together, but don't try to become one. Be together, but don't become absolutely unconnected. Remain two and yet in contact. That's what I mean by the middle. And be a little more alert. One has to be a little more conscious when one is moving in love, and one has to be careful about the other. Whatsoever you do affects that person.

Give and Take

If in a relationship one person goes on giving and the other goes on taking, both suffer. Not only the giver—because the giver feels cheated—but the person who is the receiver is also suffering because he cannot grow unless he is allowed to give. He becomes a beggar and his self-image falls low. He needs to be strengthened and he needs to be given an opportunity where he can also give. Then he feels human; he feels confident.

Not Just Sex

Be very watchful, be loving, and if sometimes sex happens as part of love, then there is nothing to be worried about. But it shouldn't be the focus. The focus should be love. You love a person, you share his being, you share your being with him, you share the space.

That is exactly what love is: to create a space between two persons, a space which belongs to neither or belongs to both—a small space between two persons where they both meet and mingle and merge. That space has nothing to do with physical space. It is simply spiritual. In that space you are not you, and the other is not the other. You both come into that space and you meet. That is what love is. If it grows, then that common space becomes bigger and bigger and bigger and then both the partners are dissolved into it.

So sometimes if you share space with somebody, a husband or friend or anybody, and sex happens as a spontaneous phenomenon—not something brooded upon, not something sought after, not something that you were planning—then it is not sexual.

There is a sort of sex which is not sexual at all. Sex can be beautiful but sexuality can never be beautiful. By "sexuality" I mean cerebral sex—thinking about it, planning it, managing, manipulating and doing many things, but the basic thing remains deep down in the mind that one is approaching a sex object.

When you look to a person through the eyes of this kind of sexuality, you reduce the other to an object. The other is no longer a person, and the whole game is only of manipulation. You are going to land in bed sooner or later. It depends how much you play with the idea and how much both of you prolong the foreplay. But if in the mind the end is just sex, then it is the sexuality I am talking about. When the mind has nothing to do with sex, then it is pure, innocent sex. It is virgin sex.

That sex can sometimes be even purer than celibacy, because if a celibate continuously thinks of sex, then it is not celibacy. When a person moves in a deep love relationship with somebody, not thinking about sex, and it happens because you share so totally that sex also comes in, then it is okay and nothing to worry about. Don't create guilt about it.

Stormy Weather

In a single moment, a person can change completely. She was so happy and she can become so unhappy. Just a moment before she was ready to die for you, and just a moment afterwards she is ready to kill you. But this is how humanity is. It gives depth, it gives surprises, it gives salt. Otherwise life would have been very tedious.

It is all beautiful. These are all notes of a great harmony. And when you love a person, you love that harmony and you accept all that makes that harmony. Sometimes it is raining, sometimes the sky is cloudy and dark, and sometimes it is full of sunlight and the clouds have disappeared. Sometimes it is very cold, and sometimes it is very hot. In just the same way, the human climate goes on changing, everything goes on changing. When you love a person, you love all these possibilities. Infinite are the possibilities, and you love all the shades and nuances.

So be true and help your partner also to be true. Then love

becomes a growth. Otherwise love can become a poisonous thing. At least don't corrupt love. It is not corrupted by hatred, remember; it is corrupted by falsity. It is not destroyed by anger, never, but it is destroyed by an inauthentic *persona*, a false face.

Love is possible only when there is freedom to be oneself without any guarding, without any reserve. One is simply flowing. What can you do? When you feel hateful, you are hateful. When the clouds are there and when the sun is shining, what can you do? And if the other understands and loves you, they will accept; they will help you to come out of the clouds because they know that this is just a climate, and it comes and goes. These are just moods, passing phases, and behind these passing phases is the reality, the spirit of the person, the soul. And when you accept all these phases, by and by glimpses of the real soul start happening to you.

Sweet Sorrow

Aloneness has in it both a sort of sadness, a sort of sorrow, and yet a very deep peace and silence. So it depends on you how you look at it.

When you are separated from your lover, look at it as a great opportunity to be alone. Then the vision changes. Look at it as an opportunity to have your own space. It becomes very difficult to have one's own space, and unless you have your own space, you will never become acquainted with your own being, you will never come to know who you are. Always engaged, always occupied in a thousand and one things—in relationship, in worldly affairs, anxieties, plans, future, past—one continuously lives on the surface.

When one is alone one can start settling, sinking in. Because you are not occupied you will not feel the way you have always been feeling. It will be different, and that difference can feel strange.

And certainly when one is separated one misses one's lovers, beloveds, friends, but this is not going to be forever. It is just a small discipline. And if you love yourself deeply and go down into yourself, you will be ready to love even more deeply because one who does not know oneself cannot love very deeply. If you live on the surface, your relationship cannot be of the depths. It is *your* relationship, after all. If you have a depth, then your relationship will have a depth.

So take this opportunity as a blessing and move into it. Enjoy it. If you become too sorrowful, the whole opportunity is wasted.

And it is not against love, remember. Don't feel guilty. In fact it is the very source of love. Love is not what is ordinarily known as love. It is not that. It is not a stew of sentimentality, emotions, feelings. It is something very deep, very foundational. It is a state of mind, and that state of mind is possible only when you penetrate your own being, when you start loving yourself. That is the meditation when one is alone: to love oneself so deeply that for the first time you become your own love object.

So in these days when you are alone, be a narcissist; love yourself, enjoy yourself! Delight in your body, in your mind, in your soul. And enjoy the space that is empty around you and fill it with love. The lover is not there—fill it with love! Spread your love around your space, and your space will start becoming luminous; it will glow. And then for the first time you will know, when your lover comes close to you, that now it is a totally different quality. In fact you have something to give, share. Now you can share your space because you *have* your space.

Ordinarily people think that they are sharing, but they don't have anything to share—no poetry in their heart, no love. In fact when they say they want to share, they don't want to give, because they don't have anything to give. They are in search of getting something from the other and the other is also in the same boat. He is searching to get something from you, and you are searching to get something from him. Both are in a way trying to rob the other of something. Hence the conflict between lovers, the tension; the continuous tension to dominate, to possess, to exploit, to make the other a means for your pleasure; somehow to use the other for your gratification. Of course we hide in beautiful words. We say, "We want to share," but how can you share if you don't have?

So enjoy this space, aloneness. Don't fill it with past memories and don't fill it with future imagination and fantasy. Let it be as it is—pure, simple, silent. Delight in it; sway, sing, dance. A sheer joy of being alone.

And don't feel guilty. That too is a problem because lovers always feel guilty. If they are alone and they are happy, they feel a certain guilt. They think, "How can you be happy when your lover is not with you?"—as if you are cheating the person. But if you are not happy when you are alone, how can you be happy when you are together? So it is not a question of cheating anybody. In the night, when nobody is looking at the rosebush, it is preparing the rose. Deep down in the earth, the roots are preparing the rose. Nobody is looking there. If the rosebush thinks, "I will show my roses only when people are around," then it will not have anything to show. It will not have anything to share, because whatever you can share has first to be created, and all creativity arises out of the depths of aloneness.

So let this aloneness be a womb, and enjoy and delight in it; don't feel that you are doing something wrong. It is a question of attitude and approach. Don't give it a wrong interpretation. It need not be sorrowful. It can be tremendously peaceful and blissful. It depends on you.

The Fire Test of Truth

No relationship can truly grow if you go on holding back. If you remain clever and go on safeguarding and protecting yourself, only personalities meet, and the essential centers remain alone.

Then just your mask is related, not you. Whenever such a thing happens, there are four persons in the relationship, not two. Two false persons go on meeting, and the two real persons remain worlds apart.

Risk is there. If you become true, nobody knows whether this relationship will be capable of understanding truth, authenticity; whether this relationship will be strong enough to stand in the storm. There is a risk, and because of it, people remain very guarded. They say things which should be said; they do things which should be done. Love becomes more or less like a duty. But then the reality remains hungry, and the essence is not fed. So the essence becomes more and more sad. The lies of the personality are a very heavy burden on the essence, on the soul. The risk is real, and there is no guarantee for it, but I will tell you that the risk is worth taking.

At the most, the relationship can break, at the most. But it is better to be separate and to be real rather than being unreal and together because then it is never going to be satisfying. Benediction will never come out of it. You will remain hungry and thirsty, and you will go on dragging, just waiting for some miracle to happen.

For the miracle to happen you will have to do something, and that is start being true, at the risk that maybe the relationship is not strong enough and may not be able to bear it. The truth may be too much, unbearable, but then that relationship is not worthwhile. So that test has to be passed.

Once you are true, everything else becomes possible. If you are false—just a facade, a painted thing, a face, a mask—nothing is possible. Because with the false, only false happens; with the truth, truth.

I understand your problem. That is the problem of all lovers: that deep down they are afraid. They go on wondering whether this relationship will be strong enough to bear truth. But how can you know beforehand? There is no a priori knowledge. One has to move into it to know it.

How are you to know, sitting inside your house, whether you will be able to withstand the storm and the wind outside? You have never been in the storm. Go and see. Trial and error is the only way—go and see. Maybe you will be defeated, but even in that defeat you will have become stronger than you are right now.

If one experience defeats you, and another, and another—by and by, the very going through the storm will make you stronger and stronger and stronger. A day comes when one simply starts delighting in the storm, one simply starts dancing in the storm. Then the storm is not the enemy. That too is an opportunity—a wild opportunity—to *be*.

Remember, *being* never happens comfortably; otherwise it would have happened to all. It cannot happen conveniently; otherwise everybody would have their own, authentic being without any problem. *Being* happens only when you take risk, when you move into danger. And love is the greatest danger there is. It demands you totally.

So don't be afraid, go into it. If the relationship survives truth, it will be beautiful. If it dies, then too it is good because one false relationship has ended, and now you will be more capable of moving into another relationship—truer, more solid, more concerning the essence.

Never Ask for Sympathy

Just be happy. A relationship is not as important as your being happy. And if you are happy, who bothers about a relationship?

A relationship is not creative, it simply reflects what is the case. It is like a mirror: if there is something to be reflected, the mirror reflects. If there is nothing to reflect, the mirror cannot create anything; it is passive. So always remember to be happy, enjoying, and if something comes by the way, good. And it *is* going to come, because a happy person has to share. But he has to wait a little, because a happy person attracts only another happy person.

If you are unhappy, you will attract many people, because they are also unhappy and something fits. There is a messiah, a therapist in everybody. So when you are in misery somebody comes and sympathizes and feels very good, high. Somebody is in misery and he is the one to help; he feels very egoistic about it. So that's how people become interested in each other. Somebody is in pain, somebody is in suffering; that person will attract many sympathizers, lovers, friends.

They will be of many sorts. They may be sadists who are interested in others being miserable. A great majority of sadists exists in the world! Or, they may be just on their ego trips. Any unhappy person helps them to feel happy in comparison, relatively speaking, so they always like to have unhappy people around them. That is the only way they know.

Remember, sympathy is not love, and if somebody is sympathetic to you, beware! It is not love, and the sympathy will remain only as long as you remain in misery. Once you become happy, the sympathy will disappear, because sympathy cannot go uphill. It is just like water flowing downhill; it goes towards people who are more unhappy than you. Sympathy never rises, it cannot rise. It has no pumping system; your sympathy cannot move towards a higher person than you.

So never ask for sympathy, because that is corrupting to you and to the other also. And if you become settled with sympathy and you start thinking that this is love, you have settled with something like a false coin. It just gives one the feeling of love; it is not love.

True love is not sympathetic. True love is *empathetic*. It is empathy, not sympathy. Sympathy means, "You are miserable, and I would like to help you. I remain outside. I give you my hand. I am not affected by you. In fact deep down I enjoy it. I relish it that one person is giving me the opportunity to feel so high." This is violent.

Empathy is totally different. Empathy means, "I feel just as you are feeling. If you are miserable, I feel your misery. It touches me, it affects me. Not as an outsider but as if I am part of your being."

Love is empathy, it is not sympathy at all.

So remember this, and resist the temptation to ask for sympathy. That temptation is there, because when one feels that love is not happening, one starts settling for less. One starts moving around in sadness and asking for sympathy in subtle ways. Never ask that. That is the greatest degradation that can happen to a human being. Never do that. Be happy.

It will take a little time for the love to happen, because most people are sadists, miserable themselves and trying to prove that they are messiahs, helpers, solving other people's miseries. But if you are happy, you will attract somebody who is not caught up in all these neurotic trips; who is simply happy and would like to share with you.

And this is the beauty of it: if you are happy and a relationship happens, you feel good, you share, but you are not dependent on it. You don't become a slave, you don't become addicted to it, because you can be happy without it.

A good relationship is a sharing; there is no dependence. Both partners remain totally free and independent. Nobody possesses, there is no need. It is a free gift. I have so much, so I give it to you. There is no need, I can be alone and perfectly happy. When two persons are in love and both can be alone and happy, then a tremendously beautiful love happens, because they are not hindering each other in any way in their growth.

Be Aware in the Moment

Whenever there is a change, any sort of change, things will come into focus more clearly. When change disturbs you, all your inner disturbances are stirred up. When you are both feeling disturbed, and both are trying to throw the responsibility on the other, just try to see it. Inside yourself, try to see it; the other is never responsible. Remember that as a mantra: The other is never responsible.

Just watch it, just watch it. And if you become wise in the moment, there will be no problem. Everybody becomes wise only when the moment is gone, and retrospective wisdom is worthless. When you are picking on something in the other person, at that very moment become aware, and let your awareness function. Immediately you will drop it.

But when you have done everything, and fought and nagged and bitched, and then later on you become wise and see that there was no point in it, it is too late. It is meaningless, you have done the harm. This wisdom is just pseudo-wisdom. It gives you a feeling as if you have understood. That is a trick of the ego. This wisdom is not going to help. When you were doing the thing, at that very moment, simultaneously, the awareness should arise and you should see that it is useless.

If you can see it when it is there, then you cannot do it. One can never go against one's awareness, and if one goes against it, that awareness is not awareness. Something else is being mistaken for it.

So remember, the other is never responsible for anything. It is something boiling within *you*. And of course the one you love is closest to you. You cannot throw it on some stranger passing on the road, so the closest person becomes the place where you go on throwing and pouring your nonsense. But that has to be avoided, because love is very fragile. If you do it too much, if you overdo it, love can disappear.

The other is never responsible. Try to make this such a permanent state of awareness in you that whenever you start finding something wrong with the other, you will remember it. You will catch yourself red-handed, and drop it then and there.

ONLY LOVE REMAINS

Only after you have moved in deep love and the ego has really been dropped—and there is something very valuable which can be gained only if you drop the ego, and that price has to be paid—when you have really loved deeply, then a new kind of integration will arise in you.

Love does two things: first it takes the ego away, then it gives you the center. Love is a great alchemy.

There are three kinds of love. I call them love one, love two, love three. The first love is object-oriented; there is an object of love. You see a beautiful woman, really graceful, with a proportionate body. You are thrilled. You think you are falling in love. Love has arisen in you because the woman is beautiful, because the woman is nice, because the woman is good. Something from the object has stirred love in you. You are not really the master of it; the love is coming from the outside. You may be a very unloving person, you may not have the quality, you may not have that benediction, but because the woman is beautiful you think love is arising in you. It is object-oriented.

This is the ordinary love, this is what is known as eros. It is lust. How to possess this beautiful object? How to exploit this beautiful object? How to make it your own? But remember, if the woman is beautiful she is not only beautiful for you, she is beautiful for many. So there will be many people falling in love with her. And there is going to be great jealousy, competition, and all kinds of uglinesses that come into your love, into your so-called love.

The story is that Mulla Nasruddin married a very ugly woman, the ugliest possible. Naturally the friends were puzzled and they asked Mulla, "You have money, you have prestige, you could have got any beautiful woman that you wanted, why have you chosen this ugly woman?"

He said, "There is a reason for it. I will never suffer from jealousy. This woman will always be faithful to me. I cannot believe anybody falling in love with her. In fact, even I am not in love with her. It is impossible. So I know nobody can love her."

With orthodox Mohammedans it is a tradition that a wife has to remain behind a purdah, behind a veil; she cannot show her face to everybody. And the new wife has to ask the husband, "To whom can I show my face and to whom am I not allowed to show my face?"

So when this woman asked Nasruddin, "To whom can I show my face and to whom am I not allowed to show it," he said, "You can show it to everybody except me!"

If you are falling in love with a beautiful woman or a beautiful man, you are getting into trouble. There is going to be jealousy, there is going to be murder, there is going to be something. You are in trouble. And from the very beginning you will start trying to possess the person so that there is no possibility of anything going wrong, or beyond your control. You will start destroying the woman or the man. You will stop giving freedom. You will encroach on the person from all sides and try to close all the doors.

Now, the woman was beautiful because she was free. Freedom is such an ingredient in beauty that when you see a bird on the wing in the sky, it is one kind of bird, but if you see the same bird in a cage it is no longer the same. The bird on the wing in the sky has a beauty of its own. It is alive. It is free. The whole sky is his. The same bird in a cage is ugly. The freedom is gone, the sky is gone. Those wings are just meaningless now, a kind of burden. They remain from the past and they create misery. Now this is not the same bird.

When you fell in love with the woman, she was free; you fell in love with freedom. When you bring her home you destroy all possibilities of being free, but in that very destruction you are destroying the beauty. Then one day suddenly you find that you don't love the woman at all, because she is beautiful no more. This happens every time. Then you start searching for another woman and you don't see what has happened; you don't look at the mechanism, at how you destroyed the beauty of the woman.

This is the first kind of love, love one. Beware of it. It is not of much value, it is not very significant. And if you are not aware, you will remain trapped in love one.

Love two is: the object is not important, your subjectivity is. You are loving so you bestow your love on somebody. But love is your quality, it is not object-oriented. The subject is overflowing with the quality of love, the very being is loving. Even if you are alone you are loving. Love is a kind of flavor to your being.

When you fall in love, the second kind of love, there is going to be greater joy than the first. And you will know—because this love will know—how to keep the other free. Love means to give all that is beautiful to the beloved. Freedom is the most beautiful, the most cherished goal of human consciousness; how can you take it away? If you love a woman really, or a man, the first present, the first gift, will be the gift of freedom. How can you take it away? You are not the enemy, you are the friend.

This second kind of love will not be against freedom, it will not be possessive. And you will not be worried very much that somebody else also appreciates your woman or your man. In fact, you will be happy that you have a woman whom others also appreciate, that you have chosen a woman whom others also desire. Their desire simply proves that you have chosen a diamond, a valuable being, who has intrinsic value. You will not be jealous. Each time you see someone looking at your woman with loving eyes you will be thrilled again. You will fall in love with your woman again through those eyes.

This second kind of love will be more a friendship than lust, and it will be more enriching to your soul.

And this second kind of love will have one more difference. In the first kind of love, the object-oriented, there will be many lovers surrounding the object, and there will be fear. In the second kind of love there will be no fear and you will be free to bestow your love not only on your beloved, you will be free to bestow your love on others too.

In the first, the object will be one and many will be the lovers. In the second, the subject will be one and it will be flowing in many directions, bestowing its love in many ways on many people, because the more you love, the more love grows. If you love one person, then naturally your love is not very rich; if you love two, it is doubly rich. If you love many, or if you can love the whole of humanity, or you can love even the animal kingdom, or you can love even trees, the vegetable kingdom—then your love goes on growing. And as your love grows, you grow, you expand. This is real expansion of consciousness. Drugs only give you a false idea of expansion; love is the basic ultimate drug that gives you the real idea of expansion.

And there is a possibility: Albert Schweitzer has talked about "reverence for life," all that lives is to be loved. Mahavira in India has said the same thing. His philosophy of *ahimsa*, nonviolence, says to love all that lives. And there is the possibility to take even one step further than Mahavira and Schweitzer. One can have reverence for things, too. That is the ultimate in love. You don't only love that which lives, you love even that which simply exists. You love the chair, the shoes, the door through which you enter your house, the plates on which your food is served. You love things, too, because they also have a kind of being. When one has come to this point that you love the whole of existence irrespective of what it is—that love becomes unconditional. It is turning into prayerfulness, it is becoming a meditation.

The first love is good in the sense that if you have lived a loveless life it is better than no love. But the second love is far better than the first and will have less anxiety, less anguish, less turmoil, conflict, aggression, violence. The second kind of love will be more of a love than the first kind, it will be more pure. In the first, the lust is too great and it spoils the whole game, but even the second love is not the last. There is love three—when subject and object disappear.

In the first type of love the object is important; in the second the subject is important. In the third there is transcendence. One is neither a subject nor an object, and one is not dividing reality in any way: subject, object, knower, known, lover, loved. All division has disappeared. One is simply love.

Up through the second type of love you are a lover. When you are a lover something will hang around you like a boundary, like a definition. With the third, all definition disappears. There is only love; you are not. This is what Jesus means when he says, "God is love"—love three. If you misunderstand the first, you will never be able to interpret rightly what Jesus' meaning is. It is not even the second, it is the third. God is love. One is simply love. It is not that one loves, it is not an act, it is one's very quality.

It is not that in the morning you are loving and in the afternoon you are not loving—you *are* love, it is your state. You have arrived home. You have become love. Now there is no division. All duality has disappeared.

The first kind of love is "I-it." The other is taken as a thing. That's what Martin Buber calls it, "I-it." The other is like a thing that you have to possess. "My" wife, "my" husband, "my" child, and in that very possession you kill the spirit of the other.

The second kind of love Martin Buber calls "I-thou." The other is a person. You have respect for the other. How can you possess somebody you respect? But Martin Buber stops at the second; he has no understanding about the third. He goes up to "I-thou," and it is a great step from "I-it" to "I-thou." But it is nothing compared to the step that happens from "I-thou" to no dualism, to oneness, where only love remains.

Even "I-thou" is a bit of a tension-creating phenomenon. You and the beloved are separate, still, and all separation brings misery. Unless one becomes totally one with the beloved, with the loved one, some kind of misery is bound to remain lurking by the side. In the first the misery is very clear, in the second the misery is not so clear; in the first it is very close, in the second it is not so close; it is far away, but it is there. In the third it is no more.

So I would like you to learn more of love. Move from the first to the second and keep it in your consciousness that the third is the goal. With the second kind of love it is a question of being. You love. You love as many people as are available. And you love in different ways: somebody you love as your wife, somebody you love as your friend, somebody you love as your daughter, somebody you love as your sister, somebody as your mother. And it is possible also that you can share one kind of love with many people. So first attain to the second kind of love.

And with the third kind of love, you are simply love. Then you can go on loving, there is no end to it.

ABOUT THE AUTHOR

Osho's teachings defy categorization, covering everything from the individual quest for meaning to the most urgent social and political issues facing society today. His books are not written but are transcribed from audio and video recordings of extemporaneous talks given to international audiences over a period of thirty-five years. Osho has been described by the London *Sunday Times* as one of the "1000 Makers of the 20th Century" and by American author Tom Robbins as "the most dangerous man since Jesus Christ."

About his own work Osho has said that he is helping to create the conditions for the birth of a new kind of human being. He has often characterized this new human being as "Zorba the Buddha"—capable both of enjoying the earthy pleasures of a Zorba the Greek and the silent serenity of a Gautam Buddha. Running like a thread through all aspects of Osho's work is a vision that encompasses both the timeless wisdom of the East and the highest potential of Western science and technology.

Osho is also known for his revolutionary contribution to the science of inner transformation, with an approach to meditation that acknowledges the accelerated pace of contemporary life. His unique "Active Meditations" are designed to first release the accumulated stresses of body and mind, so that it is easier to experience the thought-free and relaxed state of meditation.

OSHO INTERNATIONAL MEDITATION RESORT

The Osho Meditation Resort is a place where people can have a direct personal experience of a new way of living with more alertness, relaxation, and fun. Located about 100 miles southeast of Mumbai in Pune, India, the resort offers a variety of programs to thousands of people who visit each year from more than one hundred countries around the world.

Originally developed as a summer retreat for Maharajas and wealthy British colonials, Pune is now a thriving modern city that is home to a number of universities and high-tech industries. The Meditation Resort spreads over forty acres in a tree-lined suburb known as Koregaon Park. The resort campus provides accommodation for a limited number of guests, and there is a plentiful variety of hotels nearby and private apartments available for stays of a few days up to several months.

Resort programs are all based in the Osho vision of a qualitatively new kind of human being who is able both to participate creatively in everyday life and to relax into silence and meditation. Most programs take place in modern, air-conditioned facilities and include a variety of individual sessions, courses, and workshops covering everything from creative arts to holistic health treatments, personal transformation and therapy, esoteric sciences, the

Zen approach to sports and recreation, relationship issues, and significant life transitions for men and women. Individual sessions and group workshops are offered throughout the year, alongside a full daily schedule of meditations.

Outdoor cafes and restaurants within the resort grounds serve both traditional Indian fare and a choice of international dishes, all made with organically grown vegetables from the commune's own farm. The campus has its own private supply of safe, filtered water.

See www.osho.com/resort for more information, including travel tips, course schedules, and guesthouse bookings.

FOR MORE INFORMATION

about Osho and his work, see:

www.osho.com

a comprehensive Web site in several languages that includes an online tour of the Meditation Resort and a calendar of its course offerings, a catalog of books and tapes, a list of Osho information centers worldwide, and selections from Osho's talks.

Or contact:
Osho International
New York
e-mail: oshointernational@oshointernational.com